JESUS, THE WAY

JESUS,
THE WAY

Reflections on the Gospel of Luke

Joseph G. Donders

ORBIS BOOKS
Maryknoll, New York 10545

The Catholic Foreign Mission Society of America (Maryknoll) recruits and trains people for overseas missionary service. Through Orbis Books Maryknoll aims to foster the international dialogue that is essential to mission. The books published, however, reflect the opinions of their authors and are not meant to represent the official position of the society.

Library of Congress Cataloging in Publication Data

Donders, Joseph G.
  Jesus, the way.

  1. Bible. N.T. Luke—Sermons. 2. Jesus Christ—
Person and offices—Sermons. 3. Catholic Church—
Sermons. 4. Sermons, American. 5. Church year sermons.
I. Title
BS2595.4.D66   252'.6   79-4167
ISBN 0-88344-240-X

CONTENTS

INTRODUCTION

Luke has a very special name
for Christians.
He calls them:
"the followers of the Way."
He does not do that only once,
but several times.
In chapter nine of his "Acts,"
he reports how Saul
is trying to arrest and eradicate
"the followers of the Way."
And according to the same report
by Luke,
Paul himself explains,
later,
the kingdom of God
by calling it:
"the Way of the Lord."
     In the town of Ephesus
     so many started to follow
     the new Way
     that the economic structure
     of that old town
     and its idol trade
     were threatened.
And when,
according to our same reporter,
Luke,
Paul is facing the governor Felix
in court,

1

he says:
"I worship the God
of my ancestors
by following the Way."
Felix allowed him some freedom,
"because he, too,
was well informed
about the Way."
>This book reflects
>on that Way of the Lord
>by Luke.
>It is, however,
>not only a "reflection."
>It is the expression
>of what happened
>when a student community
>in East Africa
>tried to read the road signs
>on that Way of the Lord.
It is a book of sermons
based on the Sunday-readings cycle
of the liturgical year-C.
>Not all the Gospel readings
>during that liturgical year
>are from Luke;
>eleven times they are taken from John.
>Three times the sermon
>is not on the Gospel text,
>but on another reading
>of the Sunday.
>Twice the text chosen
>was from Luke's other book,
>"the Acts of the Apostles,"
>and once from Saint Paul's letter
>to the Corinthians.
This book is dedicated
to all those who took part
in the Sunday ceremonies

at Saint Paul's University Chapel,
Nairobi, Kenya,
who made these reflections possible.
Without them,
they would not have been.

1.

OUR LIBERATION IS NEAR

(Luke 21:25–28; 34–36)

There is one time in the year
that we Christians are supposed,
in a very special way,
to prepare for the coming of the Lord.
And yet,
we Christians very often seem to be
the last ones to start our preparations.
Others start long before us.
The Voice of Kenya radio stations
started playing Christmas tunes
long before the church choirs
even were thinking of their
Christmas-carol-singing preparations.
The butchers and the bakers
displayed their signs:
"Order now for Christmas"
ages ago.
> We are late;
> we are the last ones;
> it is as if we in our churches
> got into serious time-problems.

Our synchronization broke down,
our time perspective collapsed,
and our watches
with their modern date indicators
don't seem to work.
And if we read our texts today,
the confusion seems still to be
greater.
Jeremiah rightly said in his days:
   "The days are coming
   that I will send you a savior."
Paul very surprisingly for his days wrote:
   "Be ready
   when the Lord comes."
And Jesus, who came ages ago, says:
   "I am coming."
When I told a child this morning:
   "Listen,
   in four weeks time,
   Jesus, the Savior, will be born
   in this world,"
she shrugged her shoulders
and said:
   "But that happened
   long ago,
   almost two thousand years
   ago."
       And indeed,
       he came two thousand years ago,
       the one for whom people had been looking
       all through the Old Testament,
       the one who was going to redeem
       and to liberate this world,
       the one who was going to turn it,
       according to the prophecies of Jeremiah
       and so many others,
       into a place of justice and integrity.
   He came two thousand years ago

to sow, as he said himself,
a new seed,
a new life;
he came two thousand years ago
full of
>   promises,
>   miracles,
>   ideals,
>   plans,
>   justice,
>   brotherhood,
>   and even food
>   and drink
>   for all.
But what happened after his coming?
What really did happen to him
and this world?
How far are we
after those two thousand years?
>   In certain regions
>   in this world,
>   people only started to hear about him
>   eighteen hundred years later.
>   He had told his followers
>   insistently,
>   to bring his message through
>   to everyone
>   immediately,
>   but when it finally came
>   it was in a sense
>   almost too late.
When the message ultimately
came through
it showed signs
of having been stored up
for too long.
His person was still there,
that is true,

in the center of the message,
but that was practically all.
That person had been caught
and colored
in all kinds of customs and traditions.
His message had been
    interpreted,
    adapted,
    accommodated,
    rationalized,
    defended,
    and worked out
    so frequently,
that the real HE
of the story,
JESUS CHRIST,
often remained hidden
under the dust
of all those centuries
in strange and far away countries,
in quaint and long ago ages.
He had got
    the taste,
    the color,
    and the smell
    of the place
    where they had stored him
    for so long.
And you know
what happened
then,
and it is very good
that we know it.
You know how imperialism,
colonization,
cultural interference,
and the ethical revolution
preached in the name of Jesus,

broke down the African traditional system,
how they did away with the traditional
family organization,
>the core,
>the heart,
>and the backbone
>of any society,
>but especially of
>African society.
Visions of desolation,
visions of crumbling values,
visions of signs
in the sun
and in the moon
and in the stars,
nations in agony,
the powers of heaven shaken,
the spirits and ancestors upset.
>The visions Jesus had
>when speaking about this world
>and about the end of it.
>That Jesus,
>who once had said:
>"I came to bring peace,"
>and that same Jesus,
>who once had said:
>"Don't think that I came to bring
>peace,
>I came to bring
>>a sword,
>>a melting pot,
>>a hot furnace,
>>fire,
>>an oven,
>>to cast a new humanity.
"When these things
begin to take place,
stand erect,

hold your heads high,
because your liberation
is near at hand."
    And we in advent time,
    in this "he-is-coming-time,"
    are looking forward to that;
    aren't we?

2.

THE REAL TEST IS GOING TO BE THAT CHILD

(Luke 3:1–6)

Today is the Second Sunday of Advent,
the second Sunday of our preparations for Christmas,
the second Sunday of our being on the lookout for
a child.
    It is also the first Sunday
    of that grim prophet John,
    who announces that all the old things
    are going to disappear:
    the old tree will be cut,
    the axe is at the root,
    the fire is ready,
    the winnowing fan is in his hand,
    the end of this world is near,
    the child is going to come.
It is obvious that John
wants them to change,
he wants them to change their hearts,
he wants them to change this world.

And that is, I think,
the hope and desire of many of us
who are living in these days.
There are so many problems besieging us,
in this world
in this country,
in our families,
in matters religious,
in our communities
and churches.
We are hoping so much,
and we hardly know where to start.
We can say,
as some do,
no half measures:
the whole order has to change;
but that is very often
a good excuse
to do nothing at all,
because for very many reasons
a radical change like that
is impossible
and has never taken place either.
Where should we start?
How should we start:
with a political program,
with a violent revolution,
with a red brigade,
with a new economic order,
with the breaking up of the international structures,
with the blowing up of the multinationals,
with combating God,
who before all
is the cause of it all,
and who now serves only as opium
for the suffering people?
One day the disciples stood around Jesus
with that very same question,

and they asked him,
to the brim filled with their own expectations:
what is the most important,
who is the most important,
what should we do,
where should we start?
>You know,
>I suppose,
>his answer:
>HE TOOK A CHILD,
>and he put that child in
>their center,
>and he said:
>if you do not become like a child,
>if you do not identify with a child,
>the kingdom
>and its newness is NOT
>for you.
I know how this text
has often been interpreted:
that we should be like children,
meaning
>simple,
>open-minded,
>not reflecting,
>but believing
>with starry eyes.
That interpretation is right
to a certain extent,
but there is also
that other possibility:
>maybe he wanted to say,
>that if we put the child
>in the center,
>we find the lever,
>the key,
>to the new kingdom,
>to the new world
>and to the new heaven!

The bishops of the East African countries
would also like to change everything;
they are thinking of starting
Christian grassroots communities
as a solution,
or as the solution,
to the problems of this world.
But how do you start those communities?
By praying?
Okay, and what next?
    I am convinced
    that if Jesus would turn up
    during their prayers,
    and if they would ask him
    once more:
    how should we start?
    that again
    he would take a child,
    put it in their middle
    and say:
    start with this one
    start with the CHILD,
      and you know
      as well as I do
      that if this country,
      or any other country,
      would take its children
      in the center of their interest
      such a country would change:
        the feeding programs,
        the health programs,
        the cash-crop programs,
        the schooling programs,
        the family life,
        the economic life,
        the political system,
        and a revolution would take place,
        a real revolution,
        a total changeover.

We very often say
that this society
should change;
we very often speak about the rift
between the rich and the poor.
But we very often overlook
the largest marginal group
in this world:
CHILDREN.
    Christ
    suggested that we should take them
    as our most important issue,
    as it was done in every well-organized
    African society.
Maybe that is why he,
Jesus,
was born among us
as a child,
and that he did not descend as an adult.
We should be,
these days of advent,
on the lookout
for a child,
and the real test of our life
will be that
CHILD.

3.

ONLY WITH WATER

(Luke 3:10–18)

The story of John the Baptist
had been going all through the country,
and consequently more and more people
started to turn up.
They came from all sides,
in the morning,
in the afternoon,
in the evening,
and even during the night.
> They wanted to be cleansed,
> they wanted to be healed,
> they wanted to be touched,
> they wanted to be washed,
> they wanted to be baptized.
And he was
> baptizing,
> baptizing,
> baptizing,
> until he got a stiff arm,
> like someone who did not stop
> cutting grass in time.

He had become a fashion.
Ladies in Jerusalem
talked about him
in their parlors:
"Have you been there?"
"Did you see him?"
"Did he talk to you?"
"Did he baptize you?"
And men,
gentlemen from Jerusalem,
were seen walking in the sun
for hours
in order to see him.
　　John was definitely a man
　　who corresponded to a need.
　　People had been hoping so much
　　and so long
　　for a change,
　　for a real change.
　　And when they saw him at work,
　　baptizing in the river Jordan,
　　they again started to hope.
As the Gospel says:
*"A feeling of expectancy
had grown among the people!"*
　　John gave himself completely
　　to his task
　　and his mission.
　　He did not come only for one evening
　　to address an enormous crowd
　　in Uhuru Park.*
　　He did not turn up
　　only on Sundays
　　or on the holy days of obligation
　　addressing smaller crowds.
　　He was there,
　　day and night,
　　with all those people,

washing off sins,
sins,
he knew
he could NOT wash off.
He worked with a symbol,
with a prophetic sign,
and they thought
that it was
THE thing.
He knew that
what he was doing
was like washing wounds
due to poisoned blood—
washing them externally
without being able to do anything
about the poisoning internally,
without being able to do anything
about the poisoned blood.
His task was only to prepare,
his task was only to warn,
his task was very external.
He could not reach the cause,
he could not really touch sin
and the poisoning
and the human disorientation
itself.
They asked him:
"What should we do?"
The gentlemen from Jerusalem asked,
the ones who had parked their chariots
and horses outside
along the river
under the trees;
the ladies from Jerusalem asked,
and he said:
"If you have two pairs of trousers,
you must share with the one
who has none;

and if you have something to eat,
share with the one
who has nothing."
The local city-council administrators came
and some officials from the customhouse,
and they too asked:
"What should we do?"
and he said:
"Ask no more than the rate,
and don't put it in your own pockets,
no bribes,
no buttering,†
no nonsense."
And the soldiers and the policemen,
who were sent to keep order,
came also to him,
and they too asked:
"What about us,
what should we do?"
and he said:
"No intimidation,
no extortion,
no violence,
be satisfied with your regular pay."
But it was just as if,
when saying all this,
he said it
without too much conviction.
He could give that advice;
he could
wash,
purify,
warn;
he could
patch up,
amend,
repair;

he could
    recommend,
    advise,
    and urge,
but it was as when one
pours oil and spices
over a food
that remains inedible.
    He was not the Christ;
    he could not change man;
    he could baptize
    only with water.
    And that is why
    he started to insist,
    more and more:
    "Do not think that it is me;
    do not think that I will be able
    to change you,
    I baptize only with water.
    Someone else is going to come after me;
    he really will baptize you,
    he is really going to change you,
    he will pour his fire in you,
    he will change your mind,
       and your heart,
       and your soul,
       and your body."
    He insisted:
    "Please, forget about me,
    let me get smaller and smaller,
    let me be forgotten,
    it is HE who is going to change
    all and everything,
    because it is HE
    who is going to change YOU."
And in the end
they came to arrest him,

and he got smaller
as he had asked,
because they chopped off his head
and put it on a silver tray
carried by a beautiful girl,
who up to then
never had used any head at all.
He lost his head
because of the sin
he had not been able to eradicate.

    Saint John was right;
    this world can change
    only if people change their minds
    and their ways.
    Saint John was right;
    it is only fire and spirit
    that is going to do it.

FIRE AND SPIRIT:
let us be willing
to receive them,
let a feeling of expectancy
grow among us
during these days
of the coming of the
LORD.

*Uhuru Park, one of the main parks in Nairobi, where evangelists such as Billy Graham address the crowds.
†Slang for bribing.

4.

AN ANGELIC ORDER: REJOICE

(Luke 1:39–44)

In the days of Christmas
we live under a special type of obligation.
We should feel happy.
Normally we tell our children
that they should be happy and merry:
    "Do not put on that face,
    don't sulk,
    stop crying,
    blow your nose,
    dry your eyes,
    don't stand there in that corner,
    go outside
    with the others
    and play,
    what is wrong with you?"
Children always live
under that heavy obligation
imposed on them by us, adults,
to be happy and joyful,

just as we expect
that young and beautiful girls
should smile always
and under all circumstances,
though the liberated ones
do not seem to do it any more.
> But in these days of Christmas
> everybody lives under that obligation;
> we admonish each other,
> we exhort each other,
> we phone each other,
> we send letters, cards, and telegrams,
> all saying
> and repeating over and over again:
> Happy Christmas,
> merry christmas,
> be happy, happy, happy,
> happy and merry,
> rejoice,
> a child has been born to us.
We are supposed to be
as happy
as we ask our children to be.
> All this belongs to the season,
> it really belongs to it.
> It was triggered off by an archangel
> named Gabriel.
>> (If you don't believe in angels,
>> you miss a lot;
>> we are not the only intelligent beings
>> in this universe,
>> you know.)
> Gabriel started it all,
> being, so to speak,
> the first ever Christmas card,
> by announcing
> the first Christmas season
> in that small village, Nazareth,

around the 25th of March,
now almost nine months ago.
His first words were:
REJOICE.
Mary had to be happy,
she was put under that obligation,
she was addressed in something like
an imperative:
rejoice.
    But that command,
    that order,
    fell away
    against her embarrassment
    and against her response.
There is not a single indication
that she rejoiced
on the spot.
In fact
there are very many indications
that her difficulties increased
straightaway,
even difficulties in her home,
around her own kitchen table
with Joseph.
Joseph had to receive
several angelic messages
in order to keep the two
together.
And even after Joseph had been informed,
she remained alone,
believing that the promise
made to her by God
would be fulfilled.
    The world around her remained the same,
    and the people around her
    remained the same too,
    though they were rather curious
    about the swelling of her womb,

and though they were looking
kind of mischievously
at Joseph.
In her fourth month
she decided to leave
to visit and to assist her aunt,
who was then in her ninth month,
according to the message
from that same archangel,
Gabriel.
She walked through towns and villages,
alongside roads and over rivers,
she passed hundreds and hundreds of people,
men and women,
and nobody took notice of her.
All was the same,
    until she met her aunt Elizabeth,
    and even Elizabeth did not notice
    anything by herself.
    It was the baby in her womb,
    that strange prophet John,
    who suddenly filled up
    with Holy Spirit,
    and who kicked her with such a force
    that she gave a loud cry,
    and she, the old lady,
    said to her niece,
    that very young girl:
    "Blessed is the fruit of YOUR womb,
    blessed be the mother of MY Lord,
    blessed be you."
And it is only at that moment
that Mary
obeys the command to rejoice;
she suddenly bursts out in joy;
all the spiritual fireworks
that had been hidden in her
exploded,
because now she knew:

he was recognized,
   and she was recognized,
and in her joy
she saw suddenly the whole world change,
not only the situations around her,
but the whole of the human situation,
not only the conditions around her,
but the whole of the human condition,
and she too cried out in joy.
   The happiness and merriness
   of Christmas
   consists
   in seeing what Mary saw,
   in seeing what Elizabeth saw,
   in understanding
   what John kicked her about,
   in believing
   that the world is accepted,
   that we will be accepted,
   that the world will change,
   that we will change,
   in believing
   that there is a kingdom to come.
Happy Christmas
all the year through,
because this world
is with child;
its womb is filled
with a kingdom to come,
and that kingdom to come
is leaping with joy
in that very, very old womb,
much older than the womb
of Mary's elderly aunt Elizabeth.

5.

JESUS, REFUGEE IN AFRICA

(Luke 2:1–14)

It was not cold that night.
There was definitely no snow.
If there had been snow
the sheep and the shepherds
would not have been outside,
but inside,
and Joseph and Mary
would not have found
an empty stable:
all stables would have been
full.
Most probably it was so warm
that the shepherds did not even need
their traditional fires
that night.
    There was a census on,
    that is true,
    but not to count people,
    as we tell our children,
    explaining the events
    of those days.

That type of census
would have been taken
in another way,
with everybody at home.
The census taken
was of the Roman Empire.
It was a registration of land
exercise,
a kind of land-consolidation act*
in view of property taxes
to be paid.
Joseph must have had some property
near Bethlehem,
or maybe Mary,
and they had come
to have their title deeds secured.
Most probably he tried also
to profit from the occasion
to guarantee the succession rights
of the baby to be born
and his mother.
    They must have had
    sufficient property
    to justify
    that hundred-mile safari
    on foot
    together with Mary,
    who was with child.
It was not even very safe
to do so.
We wish to think that all was peaceful
that night.
Things were not peaceful at all.
In the fifth chapter of a book called
"The Acts of the Apostles"
we can read
how in the days of that very census,
and most probably because of it,

a freedom fighter,
Judas the Galilean,
had started a bloody revolt
against the Roman occupational forces.
Guerrilla fighting had been reported
all over the country.
There were infiltrators
everywhere,
the situation was tense.
It was no joke
to travel in those days.

    In Bethlehem everything
    lasted very long,
    longer than expected,
    partly because all land cases
    last longer than expected
    and partly because of the
    bureaucratic attitudes
    of the officials
    involved.
    They liked to use
    the small power given to them
    by showing it,
    by sending people from pillar to post,
    by making them go round in circles,
    by returning forms again and again
    pointing out
    that there was something missing
    or that this or that form
    should have been handed in
    in eightfold,
    and not in sevenfold only.
It was in this world
that Jesus was born,
in the midst of one of the most
hopelessly human affairs:
land affairs,

land ownership,
land registration,
and tax forms.
He descended from heaven,
into the financial worries of his parents,
almost on top of a tax form.
> And straight from there,
> when all seemed settled,
> they were seen next
> on their way
> to a refugee camp in Africa,
> in Egypt.
What a birth!
There were,
of course,
some consolations.
The angels for instance.
But even those angels behaved
rather unexpectedly.
> It was the custom
> among the Jews
> that the father was never present
> at the birth of a child.
> After the birth of the baby,
> a messenger was sent to the father
> to inform him.
> The father would then come,
> take the child on his knees,
> and accept it officially,
> giving it a name.
> Very many peoples have
> similar customs over here
> in Kenya.
> A Kamba father will do
> the very same,
> the fifth day after the birth
> of a child.

Under the circumstances
the angels should have gone to
Joseph
to tell *him:*
"A child is born to *you*,"
but instead,
they changed their flight direction,
and they flew to the shepherds
to tell *them*:
"A child is born to *you*."
>   And as those shepherds
>   represented the whole of humankind
>   that night,
>   the message is for us also:
>   "A child has been born to *you*."
From the angels' point of view,
we are now supposed
to go to the mother
of that child,
to take that child on our knees
and accept it,
giving it a name:
JESUS,
and that means:
SAVIOR.
>   Giving that name,
>   we are expressing a hope
>   that the world as it is
>   is not the world as it should be.
>   We are expressing a belief,
>   that there is KINGDOM TO COME,
>   and if we are completely sincere
>   when naming him
>   SAVIOR,
>   we are entering at the same time
>   into quite a life-program,
>   into quite a life,

the life
he himself
started in Bethlehem
that night:
a life so new
that it made him
immediately
a refugee in this world,
in Africa,
a stranger and yet
the master
of all.

*In large parts of Kenya land-ownership has been settled through a legal process called land-consolidation.

6.

FAITHFUL TO THE OLD

(Luke 2:41–52)

Today we commemorate the family
in Nazareth:
Joseph, Mary, and Jesus.
The Gospels do not tell us very much
about that family:
 after
  the angels,
  the shepherds,
  the visitors from the east,
  and the visitors from the south,
 after
  the threats of King Herod,
  the flight to Egypt,
  and their return home,
it seems that all was just normal.
Luke mentions twice
that Jesus grew,
but that is nothing special;
it is a thing babies and small boys
normally do.

Yet Mary and Joseph must have understood
that things could not remain
normal forever.
Now and then,
Mary,
looking at her son,
must have been wondering
what was going to happen to him,
and when and where.
She could not forget
the prophecies she had heard
from her aunt Elizabeth,
from the angels,
from the shepherds,
from the wise men,
from Simeon
and Anne.
    She was wondering
    when it would start,
    wondering and afraid.
Finally there was a day
with a surprise,
a day that definitely was different.
They had gone off to Jerusalem
to celebrate Easter.
The feast was over,
and they were heading for home.
She had been travelling with the women,
and Joseph with the men.
When darkness grew
they met.
She asked Joseph:
"Where is Jesus?"
At the same time he asked her:
"Where is he?"
    They asked their friends,
    their relatives;
    nobody had seen him.

They hurried back
that same night
to Jerusalem,
Joseph blaming himself,
but she wondering:
Maybe his hour has come,
perhaps it has all started.
O my God,
she prayed,
please,
not yet,
he is too young.
After a three-day boy-hunt,
after having visited all the police posts,
and all the barracks,
and all their relatives and friends,
after having asked all the streetboys
in Jerusalem,
they found him,
lost
in the temple.
Mary took him apart
and she blamed him.
She said:
"How could you do something
like that
to us?
We have been frightened for three days."
But he said:
"Why were you looking for me?
I had to be about my Father's business."
That is what he SAID,
but he went with them,
he returned to Nazareth,
and he lived there another eighteen years
under their authority.
That is what he DID.

Jesus was faithful to the new,
to the homework his father had given him
in this world.
But he was faithful to the old as well,
to the family in which he was born,
faithful to his father
and his mother,
his uncles and his aunts,
his cousins and his nieces.
He lived a double fidelity,
respecting the new and the old.
It has been said over and over again
by all kinds of experts,
by sociologists and educators,
by theologians and journalists in the local press,
that the message of Jesus Christ,
that his newness,
that his type of life
has been breaking up
the old traditional African society,
that it broke up
the old extended family
that guaranteed security to the old
and education to the young.
People introduced a new type of family,
leaving their parents alone.
Very many of the 900,000 old people in Kenya
are left alone by their children
to fend for themselves.
All this is true,
but is it true
that this could be done
in the name of Jesus?
Do you remember
how Jesus once said:
"This people honors me with their lips
but their hearts are far from me"?

And do you remember
why and when
and to whom he said this?
    He said it to condemn
    expressly and precisely
    those who used the name of God
    and their so-called dedication to God
    in order to overlook the old command:
    honor your father and your mother,
    honor your fathers and your mothers.
He told them:
    "You found a fine way
    to do away with
    the old traditional command from God:
    honor your father and your mother,
    by saying:
    I belong in a new way to God,
    declaring God's old command
    NULL and VOID."
    He even threatened them with death
    on that occasion.
It would be terrible
if that old faithfulness would fall away,
terrible for those old people,
but terrible as well for those who neglect them
and who once will be old too.
    And we cannot in truth
    appeal to God
    or appeal to Jesus Christ,
    while doing such a thing.
    Our appeal would be rejected
    and would backfire,
    scorching our own faces.
If the traditional way is done away with
not only the old ones will suffer;
the young ones are going to suffer too.
In traditional family life,
no child was uncared for,

no child would get lost,
just as Jesus did not really get lost,
because he was found by caring parents.
When the direct parents would fail or die
the family would take over,
the uncles and the aunts,
the cousins or the nieces,
and even others.
  Why is it
  that at the moment
  so many children are seen
  running loose from any family bond?
  Where is the old faithfulness,
  to one's flesh and one's blood,
  to one's life and one's growth?
It is very necessary and very useful
to speak and think
  about a traditional dress,
  about traditional music,
  about traditional dancing,
  about traditional food and drink,
  about traditional weddings and ceremonials,
  even about traditional religion,
  but we should not forget
  to be faithful to the backbone
  of human society:
  its well-ordered family life.
Jesus,
the Son of God,
broke out
once,
and even that is not true,
because he was Lord and Master of all,
but after that
he lived with them,
the divinely willed family pattern,
for thirty years,
and that is how he grew

in wisdom,
in stature,
and in favor
with God
and all the people
around him.

7.

DOES HE FUNCTION?

(John 1:1–18)

Christmas is a time
that we give each other gifts.
Everyone of us must have received
something over these days,
something small:
    a pencil,
    an eraser,
    a copybook,
    or a banana;
or something big:
    a fountain pen,
    a new pair of trousers,
    a bicycle,
    or school fees for a year.
Christmas is,
of course,
a very fitting time
for gifts.
Aren't we celebrating
the greatest gift
God ever gave to humankind,

after having given us the gift
that constituted us:
human life?
He gave his own son,
Jesus Christ.
And according to the rather
mysterious beginning
of the Gospel of today
even that first donation,
our human life,
was given to us
in him.
         Gifts—
         Jesus is a gift,
         his peace is a gift,
         his spirit is a gift,
         the three magi came with gifts,
         gifts all over
         the Christmas scene.
         In the long run,
         we risk getting so many presents
         that our house and our life
         run the risk of being overloaded
         with them.
Have a look at your home,
look around in the street,
have a look in your garden,
go once through your room,
and you will find
that all those places
are almost like cemeteries
cluttered with unused and dead things,
things on the way out.
         Cupboards,
         wardrobes,
         kitchen table drawers
         are full with old gifts
         others gave to you,

or you gave
to yourself,
that you never use:
    a miraculous potato-peeler,
    a promising pastry-maker,
    a special knife,
    some marbles from your youth,
    and so on.
You bought them, you got them,
but they did not function
and that is why they disappeared
in the dark of your room
or wardrobe.
    And this might even happen
    with that gift from God:
    Jesus Christ.
    Why did he disappear
    out of the lives of so many?
    Simply because they thought
    that he did not function.
    But why did he not function:
    because of the nature of the gift
    or because of the addressee?
If I do not want to see,
I can throw my specs away,
I can even have my eyes removed,
but am I not destined to see?
If I do not want to go forward,
I can throw my shoes away,
and if I want to be radical,
I can even have my feet amputated,
but am I not destined to
proceed?
    If I do not want to live
    in God's world,
    I can do without Jesus Christ,
    but am I not destined
    to live in his world?

In his letter to the Ephesians,
in the second reading of today,
Paul thanks his friends
not only for the fact that they
received
Jesus Christ,
but also because
he functioned in their
lives.
He wrote:
    "Having heard about your faith,
    about your faith
    in the Lord Jesus,
    and the love that you show,
    I will never fail to remember you."
That is how people
around us
should remember us
also.

8.

THE BAPTISM OF THE LORD

(Luke 3:15–16; 21–22)

After thirty long hidden years
Jesus finally appeared
from Nazareth in public.
His mother must have been waiting
for that moment.
She must have been
afraid of it as well.
In fact very many had been waiting
for that moment:
"A feeling of expectancy
had grown among the people."
    And then the morning came
    that he did leave.
    It was going to start.
    He washed his face
    for the last time at home.
    He left his room,
    he looked around in it
    and closed the door.

He greeted his mother,
who followed him to the door.
He left the house
and walked into the street.
He did not look back anymore.
He went to the nearest corner
and he chose without hesitation
his direction.
Where would he go?
To Jerusalem,
its temple,
its schools,
its learned professors
and scribes?
No,
he had been there already
as a small boy.
He had been discussing
with the theologians over there.
He had asked them for clarifications,
and he had not come further
with them.
He had examined them
for one day,
he had discussed with them
for two days,
he had tried them out
for three days,
and he had got lost,
completely lost,
lost in the temple,
with the Schillebeeckxes and the Rahners,
the Kungs, the Barths, and the Cones
of those days.
Fortunately,
two representatives from the people,
Joseph and Mary,
had come to his rescue,

and he grew up
in the daily life
of their home
with them.
 He was now
 at the corner of the street.
 To the right: JERUSALEM,
 the official church,
 the seminary,
 the Bible school,
 the books and the scrolls,
 the conferences and the symposiums,
 the updating courses,
 the refresher-days,
 the retreats,
 the consultations,
 and the pastoral center.
To the left: the crowd,
the people
on their way
to John the Baptist,
far away
from officialdom,
but full of hope,
expecting a new vision,
something to happen,
a new beginning,
salvation and redemption,
people that might be compared
with so many of the
men and women
organized in the independent churches
of this country Kenya,
those men and women with
 their registration cards,
 their flags and their drums,
 their banners and their Bibles,
 their hymns and their hopes.

He chose them;
of course, he chose them;
he had come
>   for the people,
>   for the mass,
>   for the lost,
>   for the seekers,
>   for the sinners.
He went to the left,
away from Jerusalem.
Jerusalem would come later.
Jerusalem would kill him.
He went to John
to be baptized,
identifying himself
with that crowd
around John.
>   And while he was standing there,
>   and while John poured water
>   over his head,
>   all of a sudden
>   heaven opened,
>   not over Jerusalem,
>   not over the temple square,
>   but above the broken bushes,
>   above the water and the mud,
>   above the sweat and the hope
>   of the crowd.
>   And the Holy Spirit
>   descended on him,
>   there and then,
>   in the form of
>   —can you believe it?
>   but that Spirit remained
>   in style—
>   a dove.
That was the starting-scene,
the grand opening,
the overture:

people,
not the fancy people,
but the many.
John the Baptist,
not the high priests,
but that scruffy,
rather smelly,
old fashioned
people's prophet.
And broken bushes,
mud and water,
flies and mosquitoes,
and
that
dove.

    It was all so simple,
    and it remained all so simple,
    it remained so unsophisticated
    that in the long run
    even John the Baptist
    did not understand
    anymore.

Later when he was in prison,
waiting for signs and
something terrific to happen,
he got impatient.
He finally sent his disciples
to ask him:
"Now, please, tell us,
are you the one,
or have we still to wait
for another one?
Are you the one,
or aren't you?"

    His answer was:
    "I am with the crowd,
    I am assisting the poor
    and the sick in the street,
    sinners are healed,

and people who were dead
started to walk."
And then John understood;
it had started,
because the people
were on the move.
It had started,
and it should continue.
There is still the tendency
for us Christians
to float
to what you might call
the top,
the temple top.
We want to be in,
with the elite,
with those who rule
and those who are rich.
We want to be in
with the few.
The more officially
a Christian you are,
the less you relate,
often enough,
to the many.
The many means humankind.
Let us be faithful to Jesus
and to the many,
and that means in fact
nothing but:
let us be faithful
to ourselves.

9.

1800 BOTTLES
AND HEAVEN OPEN

(John 2:1–12)

Just before he went to Cana,
Jesus had been speaking
to his brand-new disciples.
He had been telling them:
"I am telling you,
from now on,
you will see heaven open
and you will see the angels,
swinging in and out."
     And then they left for Cana.
     That first day
     they were following him
     from so near
      that they tripped
      on his heels.
At Cana,
there was his sign.
He let his glory be seen,
and they believed in him.
Heaven was open,

all its windows had been opened,
the doors were wide open.
God had started his new
OPEN HOUSE policy,
and that day,
the first day,
he gave them
a day on the house.
       What happened?
       There was a wedding feast.
       That means:
       a nervous bride,
       wrestling with almost a square mile
       of mosquito net,
       an impatient husband,
       who,
       when looking at his bride,
       wished the whole feast were over,
       very many guests,
       family and good friends,
       but also plenty of people
       who had come only to have
       a good and thorough and free booze,
       a record player in the corner,
       repeating again and again,
       that classical song: "Malaika,"*
       and everything went on very well,
       and some guests had just started
       to sing: "Drink, drink . . ."
       holding out their empty glasses
       when the news came through,
       the almost unbelievable news,
       that the wine (or the beer)
       was finished.
       And suddenly it was
       as if the whole feast
       was falling into the water,
       the only drink left in the kitchen.

Water,
who drinks water?
Definitely not the fishermen
from the lake of Galilee.
    The bride put her veil over her face,
    the bridegroom loosened his tie,
    and everybody was extremely embarrassed;
    it all seemed over.
And there is Jesus
and his mother Mary,
and she tells him:
"They have no wine,"
as if he had not noticed
that his glass,
too,
had been empty
for the last quarter of an hour.
"They have no wine."
And he said:
"Why turn to me?"
But he went to the kitchen,
and he looked around,
and he pointed at the water jars
and the empty wine casks in the corner.
And he asked them:
"Are they filled?"
And they said:
"No."
And he said:
"Fill them!"
And they filled them,
and they were wondering
whether he was really expecting them
to serve water
to the guests,
water, normally used to wash yourself
and the dishes.
But then it happened:

he turned the whole lot
into wine,
six jars of thirty gallons each.
      Do you know
      what that means?
      It means 1800 half-liter bottles;
      that is about 72 beer crates full,
      that is about 3600 glasses,
      and that means
      that if there were a hundred guests,
      18 bottles each.
      And do not forget
      that all this happened
      at the *end* of the feast.
Happy feast day to you!
The story says
that he and his mother
and his brothers
went after that to Capernaum.
It does not even mention
the disciples anymore.
I wonder how they got home.
      And all this
      was a sign.
      A sign of what?
When Mary approached Jesus,
she said:
"There is no wine,"
and Jesus said:
"But my hour has not yet come."
I think
that when Mary saw Jesus
coming to the feast,
a wedding feast,
her heart must have been
jumping up in her.
She must have been thinking:
"It is going to start,

he is going to redeem us all,
he is going to free us,
he is going to change the world,
he is going to change us."
    And when he just sat down,
    like all the others,
    she went to him,
    and she said:
    "They,"
    meaning not only the couple in question,
    but meaning humankind,
    meaning us,
    "they have nothing worth
    drinking anymore,
    they are thirsty,
    they are looking for something
    new."
    And he said,
    knowing perfectly well
    what she meant:
    "My hour has not yet come,
    it is not yet so far,
    wait."
But then,
to show that that hour would come,
to show her that she was right
in her expectations,
to show her that the final outcome
would be what she hoped for,
he went to that kitchen
and changed all that water
into all that wine
as a sign of the things
to come.
    That wine
    was the wine of the kingdom.
    It is a sign
    of the Spirit given to us.

We should drink it,
to drink joy and humanity and divinity
into our old, worn-out human existence.
We should be enlivened by it,
even up to the point
that others might say of us
what they said of Peter
when he was filled with that SPIRIT:
"Look at him,
he is drunk,
drunk so early in the morning."
All this seems easy,
but it means a switch-over
from the old to the new,
from the old person to the new person.
And once
Jesus himself warned:
"Nobody who has been drinking old wine
wants the new one;
they say:
'The old one is better.'"

*"Malaika" (Angel), a popular Swahili love song sung all over the continent.

10.

CELEBRATING OUR LIBERATION

(Luke 4:14–21)

These days of ours
are the days
that we should celebrate
our liberation,
our full liberation.
  Very many African theologians
  stress
  that the main theme of African theology
  is that theme of liberation,
  liberation from all those external
  and exterior forces
  that frustrate and handicap,
  that thwart and bind,
  liberation
  even
  from what many call these days
  the white man's religion.
There are liberation theologians,

there are liberation educators,
there are liberation psychologists,
and there are liberation counsellors,
and almost all of them,
and maybe all of them,
say
that a real liberation
can come only
from within.
    Modern counsellors
    will help their clients
    in such a way
    that the patients
    start to give the answers
    to the problems
    from within themselves.
Paulo Freire,
one of the greatest specialists
in the education
of oppressed people,
states very clearly
    that a real liberation
    cannot come from the outside.
    If it comes only from the outside,
    it is going to imprison us
    again,
    if only because our liberators
    are going to say
    that our liberation
    depended
    on them.
    Liberation and freedom
    come from within.
Let us take an example.
You are here this morning
in this chapel
for a Sunday mass.
Why are you here?

Are you here because you
have to be here?
Are you here because somebody told you
that you should be here?
Are you here because there is a
law?
Are you here because you are
afraid?
Are you here because you think
that otherwise
heaven will remain closed to you?
Are you here because of the
lawgiver?
      Or are you here
      because you love to be here,
      because you love to be here
      with all the others,
      in this company of each other,
      together with your fellow students
      and our guests
      from all over the world
      and the drums
      and the music
      and the singing,
      together with God
      and his angels
      and the flowers
      and the bread
      and the water
      and the wine
      and Jesus Christ.
I am here
because I love to be here,
and I love to be here
because you are here,
and the Spirit is here in you
and if you were not here
I would not be here either.

The two cases are different;
in the first case: constraint;
in the second case: love.
And you can see the difference.
The person who is here
because of his father
or her mother,
because of the law
or the temperature of hell,
shows that
in his or her face,
in her or his fists.
The people who are here
because they love to be here
show that freedom
too.
And it is that second case,
the case of the liberated freedom,
the liberty he came to bring
according to the Gospel of today,
that we should celebrate.
We should never forget,
that Jesus left his disciples,
after having said to them:
"It is best for you
that I leave;
if I would stay with you,
you would never live
the Spirit that is in you."
And he disappeared in the clouds,
in the light of the rising sun,
early in the morning.
They remained looking up,
they remained bound to him,
and they remained looking up,
until a couple of heavenly messenger boys
arrived on the scene
to tell them to move.

"I, Jesus,
yes,
I, Jesus,
would always be
an alienating force
from the outside;
and you,
yes,
you,
would always be
imitation men
and imitation women,
without your own
and proper identities,
without knowing about the
Spirit
in you.
        "So start to move
        and to live
        on your own.
        Everything I wanted
        to give you
        is given to you
        from within,
        from within your own community,
        from within yourselves.
        Do not forget about me,
        I am with you
        always!
        See you
        again!"

11.

HE AND HIS EXTENDED FAMILY

(Luke 4:21–30)

That sabbath day Jesus
was in the synagogue
of his hometown,
Nazareth.
And there they were all sitting
in front of him:
    his brothers
    and his sisters,
    his mother,
    his uncles and his aunts,
    and all the others
    he had known so very well
    during his thirty years
    at Nazareth.
They had heard about his baptism
by John the Baptist.
They had heard
how at the moment
of that baptism
heaven had split open,

how a voice had been heard
and how the Spirit had been seen.
They had heard how
he had disappeared into the desert,
and according to some further rumors
he had fought
in that desert
with the devil
for forty days,
and how he had
won.
       And then
       they had heard about the wine at Cana,
       1800 half-liter bottles full,
       and they had heard about
          the deaf
          and the dumb
          and the crippled
          and the blind
          and the dead.
They had been talking already
about the bread that
inevitably would come
and about the money
he was going to find anywhere,
even in the mouth of a fish.
       They did not say it.
       He himself said it,
       because he knew them so very well,
       he said:
          "And now you are going to ask me,
          what about your own people,
          what about your own family,
          what about your own mother,
          what about your brothers and sisters,
          what about your own village,
          what are you going to do
          over here
          for them?"

They were thinking
about all that
he might do for them.
Wasn't he one of theirs?
Hadn't he been to school with them?
    And the thought
    about the travellers
    who would come,
    the pilgrims and the tourists,
    and about the hotels
    they would need,
    and about the *chai-*,
    the *ugali-*,
    and the *nyama*-kiosks.*
    They thought about the
    small plots of land
    they owned
    in Nazareth,
    and about the land prices
    that would skyrocket,
    about the bread
    that would be sold,
    and about the beer
    that would be drunk.
They wanted to pin
him down
in their village,
in their location,
in his family.
They wanted to use him,
to catch him,
to fix him
in their ties of
    blood,
    tribe,
    and land.
He answered their question.
He said:

"In the days of the great prophet Elijah,
there were very many serious cases of leprosy
among the people
that considered itself
God's own people,
his chosen race,
the Jews;
but God healed only Naaman,
   a stranger,
   a foreigner,
   a non-Jew,
   an outsider,
   a barbarian,
   an expatriate,
   a *mzungu,*
   a *mgeni.*"†
Jesus refused
to be pinned down
by them;
he refused
to be restricted
by them;
he refused to be caught
in those human ties
and strings
and relations.
He was not only their son;
he was the son of God,
God who made all.
   And they understood,
   and they sprang to their feet,
   and they bared their teeth,
   and they drove him out of the synagogue,
   and they chased him up to the brow of the cliff,
   on which Nazareth was built,
   and they wanted to throw him down,
   but he saved himself from them
   that time.

They were wrong;
Jesus did not neglect his own family.
After all,
didn't he perform his first miracle
because his mother
asked him to do so?
After all,
hadn't he come to his own home village
to see them
and to help them?
They were wrong;
Jesus didn't neglect his own people.
Didn't he tell that expatriate lady
from Syro-Phoenicia
that he hadn't come for her
but for his local people?
And wouldn't he,
later on in his life
sit down on a hill
overlooking Jerusalem,
that beautiful city in the sun,
and weep,
weep
big silent tears
because his own people,
made of the flesh and blood
he was made of,
did not listen?
>   But he was not going to be tied up
>   by them
>   or to them
>   alone.
He had to be faithful
in a twofold way,
faithful to his family
but faithful as well
to humankind,
that family of God.

And he healed the Syro-Phoenician woman,
and they could not stand it;
and he sat down with the prostitutes,
and they could not stand it;
and he praised the Samaritan, that stranger,
and they could not stand it;
and he helped a Roman family,
an officer from the occupying forces,
and they could not stand it;
and he stopped their own temple-service,
in holy Jerusalem,
saying:
 "From now on
 all nations
 will be equal,"
and they sprang again
to their feet,
and they bared their teeth,
and they killed him
 that time.
And he died
for them all,
for his executioners,
for his judges,
for his people,
for you,
for me,
for all.
 They could not pin him down,
 because he did not want
 to be pinned down.
 There was nothing
 that could hold him;
 he was not for sale,
 though Judas sold him.
He did not claim
a home;
he had no house.

He did not claim
money;
Judas carried his purse.
He did not claim
a wife;
he remained unmarried.
He did not claim
a *shamba;* ‡
he is said to have said
that he hadn't even a stone
to put his head
on.
He did not claim
children;
he had no son,
he had no daughter;
but speaking about children,
he said:
"Let them ALL come
to me."

> And when he spoke to them,
> he used to sit down in a boat
> on the lake,
> on those extraterritorial waters
> claimed by no owner
> but by God.
> And even that boat
> was not his own;
> it was Peter's boat.

Jesus was faithful in a twofold way.
He was faithful to his people there
and to us, his people over here;
he was faithful to his family over there
and to his own family over here.
He was the son of Mary,
and therefore the brother of many
in Nazareth;

he was the son of God
and therefore the brother
of all
in this world.
And we should be like him.
And we will not prosper,
and this humanity will not grow,
and this world will not survive,
and this country will not be a nation,
and this university will not be a community,
and you personally will have no security
and no integrity,
and you will always risk becoming a refugee,
if this twofold fidelity
is not realized
by us:

    faithful to the many
    and faithful to all.

*chai: tea; ugali: porridge; nyama: meat.
†mzungu: white person; mgeni: stranger.
‡shamba: farming field.

12.

TOUCH AND GO

(Luke 5:1–11)

Up to that morning Peter
had not been overcome.
He had been surprised,
but no more than that.
He had not really been touched,
and he had not really decided
on what to do either.
    He had been drinking wine in Cana,
    but he was not impressed.
    He always bought his wine from somewhere
    when he needed it,
    and it had always been there in a bottle,
    when he needed it.
    He had never thought about all the work
    that goes into the making of wine.
    To Peter wine seemed easy;
    you just fill barrels with grape juice,
    you add certain things,
    you store it,
    and you wait.
    That is it,
    and that is all there is to it.

He had not even been overcome
by the fact that Jesus had thrown out
a devil
from a demoniac.
He had been astonished,
and he had been saying with the others,
"What a teaching,
and what a teacher;
he gives orders to unclean spirits,
and they obey him just like that!"
But that was all.
Nothing really struck home.
        But this fish was different.
        They had been fishing the whole night,
        and they had caught
        only a few dead crabs,
        an old sandal,
        a broken pot,
        and some pieces of firewood.
        Hopeless.
        They had already started cleaning their nets
        when he came along,
        the man of that wine at Cana,
        the man of those healing incidents.
And he,
that man,
said:
"Throw out your nets!"
And they had answered:
"Now listen,
you might be able to turn water
into wine,
but a vineyard owner
can do the same;
you might have healed some people,
right,
but a doctor does the same;
but to throw our nets out
now,

after this night,
NO!
Do you want us to make fools of ourselves
in front of all those people?
We are fishermen,
you know,
and you are not!"
    They looked at Jesus,
    they saw that he insisted,
    so Peter said:
    "Okay, we'll do it,
    let's make fools of ourselves."
    And looking at Jesus he added:
    "We're in good company!"
    And they threw out their nets.
    They splashed in the water,
    and there was suddenly a rush in that water.
    It moved all over,
    the boats were almost pulled down,
    and the nets were filled with fish,
    all kinds of fish,
    an onrush of fish:
        tilapia,
        eel,
        pike,
        and needle fish.
    Peter, almost automatically,
    evaluated the contents of the nets;
    tilapia at 35 shillings a kilo,
    eel at 45,
    needle fish at 30.
And suddenly he got touched,
suddenly it struck him,
abruptly it hit him:
he was standing in the company of God,
and he shouted out:
"Get away from me,
I am a sinful man,
go away."

Just as Isaiah
in the first reading of today
also shouted
at the moment he saw God:
"See how wretched I am,
I, a man with unclean eyes,
I saw God;
I, a man with unclean ears,
I heard God;
I, a man with dirty sinful hands,
I touched him:
   I am lost,
   let me go,
   let me die."
As the African proverbs say:
"It is no good to be too near
to a chief;
it is no good to be too near
to a king,
except when you are called,
but even such a call is
a bad sign."
   It is no good to be too near to God;
   he wants too much,
   he knows too much,
   he is too singleminded.
   It is not good to touch God;
   it is too dangerous.
   You are going to lose your LIFE;
   you are going to lose YOUR life.
   And they did.
An angel came
from behind God
to Isaiah,
who was trembling
and shaking all over,
just like a small boy
before he is going to be beaten
by his father.

And the angel took a burning coal,
a live burning coal,
and he burnt the evil out of Isaiah,
and a voice was heard,
and he was sent,
and off he went.
He lost HIS life,
and won it back in God
and his new mission.
>Peter fell on his knees;
>James fell on his knees too,
>and John as well,
>just like men condemned to death,
>pleading for their lives,
>and Jesus said:
>"Do not be afraid;
>follow me,
>and you will catch men
>together with me,
>just as I am catching you
>now."
>>And they brought their boats
>>to the shore,
>>and they arranged for the fish
>>to be sold
>>by their friends,
>>and they left everything
>>and followed him.
They lost their lives
and won new ones.
And that is the risk
we too
live under
when we live with Christ.
>And that is why it is very hard for us
>to be really with him.
>That is the reason for so many
>difficulties in our prayers.

We do not need the devil to tell us
not to pray;
our own nature tells us
not to do it.
It is too dangerous,
you are going to be caught,
you are going to be sent.
Who wants to be with him?
Who wants to open his or her heart?
Who wants to be touched?
Because to be touched
means to be sent,
to be sent by him,
who in his singlemindedness
is thinking of only one aim:
his kingdom to come.

13.

SECOND SIGHT

(Luke 6:20–26)

At first sight
the Gospel reading of today
is clear:
>Happy are the poor,
>happy are the hungry,
>happy are those who weep,
>>happy,
>>happy,
>>happy,
>>praised,
>>praised,
>>praised,
>>blessed,
>>blessed,
>>blessed.
>Woe to the rich,
>woe to those who have their fill now,
>woe to those who laugh now,
>>woe,
>>woe,
>>woe,

                warned,
                warned,
                warned,
                cursed,
                cursed,
                cursed.
It seems simple,
and also pretty harmless
to all of us,
because none of us is rich,
and the food in the university refectory
is not all that good,
and we have plenty of reasons to weep
and not so very many to laugh.
            If I would ask you in this chapel
            can the rich, please, stand up,
            nobody would stand up,
            not because the rich are shy—
            the rich are not shy about their riches—
            but because none of us
            considers himself or herself rich.
In other words,
this reading from Luke
means only that all of us
will be blessed.
            I wonder whether that was the intention
            of Jesus,
            and of Luke,
            who passed this information on
            to us?
The readings of today
are about more
than simply being rich or poor.
They are about something
Jeremiah
and Paul
mention in the first and second readings.

Jeremiah remarks:
"The man who puts his trust
only
in this world is going to be deceived."
And Paul writes:
"If our hope in Christ has been for this life
only,
we are the most unfortunate of all people."
They are about the fact
that this world is not all there is;
they are about the fact
that through this world we should see
another world to come;
they are about the fact
that in this world the kingdom of God
is finding its way.
In other words,
the readings try to warn us:
"Do not forget
that the stage you are at
now
is only a developmental stage,
a transition.
Do not forget
that you are invited to another meal
with the Father.
Do not forget that you are going to be taken
up.
Do not forget that this world is built on
loose sand,
that you will have to leave it,
in the same way you came to it.
Do not forget that you should be preparing
now,
for what is going to come."
All this
is one of the most essential parts
of Jesus' message.

He was so aware of it
that he saw this fact,
this reality,
everywhere in this world.
It was a kind of SECOND SIGHT
with him.
     He wanted to convince us,
     that we should not install ourselves
     over here,
     as if we were never going to leave
     this place.
     We are only on our way;
     we have still to be born;
     this world is like a womb
     to us,
     and what human being to be born
     would cling to the womb
     for always?
Take a woman who is pregnant;
in her womb a small human reality
is being formed.
That reality is in its
eighth month,
living in her womb
     very nicely,
     very snugly,
     very warm,
     well fed,
     sufficient moisture,
     air conditioned,
     carefully controlled,
     shockproof,
     all vitamins and minerals necessary,
     no overheating,
     no undercooling,
     well-protected in a kind of
     hotwater cushion,
     and so on.

Now just imagine that
you can come into contact
with that baby to be born,
now in its eighth month,
and you say:
"Hey, little thing,
over there inside,
four more weeks to go,
and then you will come out,
you know."
        And the little things says:
        "Coming out?
        What do you mean?
        I am fine over here,
        this is the world I know,
        this is the world I love.
        I am going to be here
        forever and ever.
        I don't believe what you
        say."
And you answer:
"Hey, little thing,
over there inside,
don't you feel your feet,
with those ten little toes,
don't you feel your hands,
with those ten little fingers,
and your eyes,
and your nose,
and your ears?
        They are to walk,
        you know,
        they are to work,
        to see,
        to smell,
        to hear,
        and your mouth is
        to suck."

And the little thing says:
"No, I do not want all that."
And it creeps deeper in the womb,
and it tries to install itself better,
at least it thinks so,
overlooking that all its growth
is in view of that new world
it is going to be born in.
It is that type of message
Jesus tried to convey to us.
And according to Saint John
he even used the very example
we just heard.
He tried to tell us,
over here inside this world,
that even this second stage of our existence,
after our first stage in that womb
of our mother
is not ALL there is,
that we should be developing now,
to be born again.
He wanted to convince us
that we should not try to install
ourselves over here,
as if we are going to remain here
forever and ever,
building big houses,
buying large tracts of land,
installing ourselves snugly
and comfortably and securely,
as if nothing is going to happen to us
anymore.
There is something else
in the coming,
and we should organize our lives
in such a way
that we take that coming world
into consideration,

using our heads
and our hands over here
in view of that final life,
that final kingdom,
that final stage,
building Christ's body,
within the womb of this world,
the body that will be born
in the world to come.
There is a very old story
about Lazarus,
the man who came out of his grave
not because
he
had asked for it,
but because
his sisters
had asked Jesus to call him
back to life.
And that very old story tells
how Lazarus could not stop laughing,
when he saw the people around him busy
building enormous houses,
discussing the latest fashions,
worrying about their security,
and taking life insurance.
He laughed
and he laughed
and he laughed;
he could not stop laughing,
up to the moment
that the villagers got so fed up
with him,
that they took him with force
and put him back in his tomb again,
sealing the tomb behind him
very carefully.

That is what so many of us did
to our second sight,
to that second sight of Jesus.
We do not want to think about it.
We install ourselves over here
as if this is all.
Let us live,
knowing what is going to come.

14.

LOVE YOUR ENEMIES

(Luke 6:27–38)

Some people say
that the Bible is old,
that it is irrelevant.
Even people who believe in Jesus
sometimes say so.
One of them wrote a short poem
that says:
>"So shut the Bible up
>and show me how
>the Christ you talk about
>is living now."

And that is what I would like to do,
to show you today,
how the Christ we talk about
is living
among us
NOW.
But how would we be able to do that
if we were not informed first
about that Christ from the Bible.

That is why
it is good
to start with a
Bible text.
Let us use the one we just read:
 "Love your enemies,
  do good to those who hate you,
  bless those who curse you,
  pray for those
  who treat you badly."
In the case of Jesus,
this was not only a question
of words.
He prayed for his executioners
while dying;
he healed
the ear of one of the people
who came to arrest him,
when Peter chopped around
with his sword,
that fatal night
that he was arrested.
 But all that happened
 long ago,
 almost two thousand years ago.
 Where is that Christ
 now?
When we then start to think
about his followers,
we are looking too often
to far off regions,
to far off cultures,
to ages ago.
 We think of saints
 and martyrs,
 confessors, virgins,
 and holy children
 there and then.

What about
here and now?
Some time ago,
a famous Ugandan author,
Taban lo Liong,
gave a speech over here in town,
in a foreign cultural center,
in the German Goethe Institute.
He said that one of the difficulties
in modern African education
is
that there seem to be
no African "models."
The "models" used
are coming from
other literatures and cultures,
from Shakespeare and from the West.
    Is that true?
    Are there no African models?
    Are there no African heroes?
    Are there no African saints?
Did you read the diary
of that Ugandan archbishop
who was killed some time ago?
Did you read it?
    In the early morning
    of Saturday, February 5, 1977,
    soldiers climbed over the fence
    around his house.
    They forced their way
    into his house.
    They threatened Archbishop Janani Luwum
    at gunpoint.
    They searched his house,
    they scared his children.
    He declared:
    "There are no arms in my house,
    we pray for the president,
    we pray for his security forces."

After the search,
two-and-a-half hours later,
they were ready to leave.
They asked him
to open the gate for them.
His wife suggested
to the archbishop:
"Don't open the gate;
let them go out
in the same way
as they came in:
over the fence!"
But he,
Archbishop Janani Luwum,
told her:
"We are Christians;
we have clean hearts,
and as a witness
we are going to open the gate
for them."
And that is
what he did.
"Love your enemies,
do good to those who hate you,
pray for those
who treat you badly."
Ten days later,
as you all will still remember,
Archbishop Janani Luwum
disappeared from among us.
He was shot.
The Christ we talked about,
living then,
dead now.
But is he really dead?
And if he is dead,
why then
do we speak about him
now?

We say:
"What a shame,
what a terrible shame
that he was killed."
Archbishops and canons
have been saying:
"What a loss,
what a terrible loss
in the African church leadership."
They are right,
and they are not right.
He disappeared,
that is true;
even his body is lost;
it was burnt and scattered
in the wind.
But is he lost?
Aren't we thinking about him
today
as an example,
as a model?
And do examples
and models not lead
us?
Archbishop Janani Luwum
decided to resist violence
in a nonviolent way.
And he won,
because of what we now
think of him
and because of what we now
think of the violence
he resisted.
In fact,
he was sure to win
all through,
because he proved to be
a son of the Most High.

The spirit of the archbishop,
the saint Janani Luwum,
will triumph,
because it is
GOD'S OWN SPIRIT.

15.

TURNING DESTINY
INTO HISTORY

(Luke 4:1–13)

For thirty years
he had been at home.
They must have been talking
about him
over there in Nazareth.
Thirty and still at home,
thirty and still with mother.
They must have been asking themselves
and each other:
"What is wrong with that chap?"
    He must have been living
    a very simple life,
    the normal life of a rather dead
    up-country location,
    with its local squibbles and squabbles,
    with now and then
    a murder,
    a suicide,
    a rape,

a scandal,
or a raid from the Roman Military Police,
because they lived unfree
in an occupied and colonized country.
But he seemed to accept all that,
just like the others,
as his fate,
the human condition,
his destiny,
something you should
and could not do anything about.
    But then he suddenly left,
    he broke out,
    he started what later would be called
    his public life.
    He left his mother.
    He left his village.
    He went out
    and the first thing he did
    was to identify
    with a group of people:
    his first companions.
He could have chosen different groups.
He could have chosen commerce,
big business,
the world of the tycoons and the hyenas,*
the world that turns stones into bread,
earth into coffee and gold,
elephant-tusks into ornaments,
money and influence.
The devil,
explicitly and personally,
asked him to do so.
He declined.
    He could have chosen the group of the politicians,
    the power-wielders,
    organizing armies,
    inviting foreign specialists,

buying military hardware.
Later,
during his trial before Pilate,
he admitted
that he would have been authorized
to call in the heavenly armies
for a big overthrow,
if he had wanted to.
The devil,
explicitly and personally,
invited him:
"I will give all the power in the world;
it is mine."
He declined.
He might have chosen the officially religious group.
Climbing to the top of the temple
and its hierarchy,
venerated by God and by man,
carried on the hands of angels.
Satan
put him at that top,
for a second or so,
and that devil pleaded:
"Accept,
you will work great things,
people will applaud you,
they will honor and bless
you."
He declined.
No commerce,
no power,
no churchmanship.
He chose another group.
He walked away from Nazareth
in the direction of John the Baptist.
And he joined there a group
of people queuing up
in front of that prophet.

He identified himself with the people
who were looking for
some more
    justice and integrity,
    humanity and spirit,
    goodness and fortitude,
    temperance and righteousness.
It is with them that he identified
in their struggle for wholeness
and holiness,
for some respect
and human dignity;
in their struggle against
slavery
and degradation
and against the cause of those evils:
exploitation and oppression.
    After his baptism in that crowd
    he went into the desert
    and he fought alone and by himself
    with those wild animals
    that wanted to devour him:
        greed,
        power,
        honor.
And he was tempted,
deeply tempted,
to forget about his choice,
to forget about
    their misery,
    their poverty,
    their smell,
    and their struggle,
    and to join the in-crowd:
    the influential ones,
    the VIP's,
    the jet-set,
    the beautiful ones.

But he stuck to his first decision;
he was seen with the poor,
with the wretched of the earth,
with sinners and prostitutes,
with the publicans and the sick,
with the stupid and the children,
and he tried to show them,
all of them,
that they should not RESIGN,
that they should not consider their state
as their fate or destiny,
but that they should enter
INTO HISTORY,
trying to develop
and to grow
and to become
real men and women,
sons and daughters of God.
    They followed him,
    and they did not follow him,
    and that was his suffering.
    They promised him,
    and they betrayed him,
    and that was his cross.
    They did move on,
    one step,
    and then moved back
    another step,
    and that was his scourging,
But he remained faithful to them,
and he still is
suffering with us
through this almost endless
human history of ours
from which we can escape
and from which we are tempted to escape
day and night:

money, money;
power, power;
honor, honor.
Student pamphlets
all over East Africa
end with:
"la luta continua,"
the fight goes on,
"solidarity with the people."
Are you serious about that?
He,
Jesus,
was,
is,
and will be.

*hyenas: a word used by the Tanzanian press to indicate capitalists.

16.

HIS SUFFERING
AND HUMAN HISTORY

(Luke 9:28–36)

When I was a child,
I went to a school,
and when I was very young,
that school was run by sisters.
During the season of Lent
the sisters said
that we were commemorating
the suffering of Jesus
and that we, children,
should suffer something too.
And we would not eat sweets
for all those weeks;
we would put them in a box
until Easter.
At Easter we ate them all,
in one go, and were sick.
    Later, I heard about all kinds of saints
    who participated in that same suffering
    of Jesus
    in very strange ways.

To give only one example:
Alphonsus of Liguori
took a vow in the year 1734
to eat only bread
and to drink only water
on Saturdays.
From 1732 to 1736
he ate his supper
sitting on the ground
with a stone around his neck,
and every morning after rising
he whipped himself for two hours,
and at the age of thirty-six
he decided never to shave,
and that must have been quite something,
because he became ninety-one.
He broke that vow
of non-shaving
three times,
forced by the people
he was living with,
for reasons that need
no explanation.
We were invited to do the same,
not exactly the same,
but to do things like that.
Some of my friends,
would walk with stones
in their shoes
for miles and miles
on a pilgrimage;
others wore hairshirts
or painful bracelets
around their arms.
    Today
    we are inclined to laugh
    at all this.
    Why do even Christians
    laugh at it?

I think it is
because we all consider
that kind of self-inflicted suffering
ridiculous in our present-day world.
We think it ridiculous
because it is artificial.
And it is artificial
because it does not seem
to have ANYTHING to do
with the suffering of Jesus Christ.
At least that is
what I think.
I think that it has no relation
to the suffering of Jesus.
Alphonsus thought it did,
and he practiced that, his belief,
in an astonishingly heroic way.
I admire the way
in which he was faithful to his insight,
but I do not admire
his insight.
    In the Gospel reading of today,
    Jesus is on the top of Tabor,
    discussing with Moses and Elijah
    his passover,
    his exodus.
    He spoke with them
    about his suffering.
    He spoke about it
    with Moses,
    who had suffered so much
    while guiding his stubborn people
    out of Egypt.
    He consulted Elijah,
    who had suffered so much
    when he had tried to bring
    that same stubborn people
        —one day hobbling on their right leg:
        faithful to God,

another day hobbling on their left leg:
   worshipping Baal—
back to their God.
In this context
it is obvious
that Jesus was speaking not only
about his exodus,
that he was thinking not only
about himself,
but about humankind also
and about the almost endless way
he would have to go with us,
escaping from the chaos
in which we are living,
a chaos that sometimes
seems organized,
but a chaos
that coexists with us
and that now and then suddenly erupts
and stones fly
and guns are fired
and breadvans are turned over.
   When we read the papers
   these days,
   it is the same sad tale
   all over the world,
   a tale of people
   struggling and suffering,
   a tale of bloodshed and violence,
   of murder and rape,
   of crime
   and throw-away children,
   and it is in that environment
   that Jesus placed himself
   when queuing up
   in front of John the Baptist,
   when fighting his temptations,
   when discussing with Moses and Elijah
   his passover.

The real suffering of Jesus
was his participation
in human history.
His real suffering was,
as he said himself to his followers,
according to Luke 9:45:
to be handed over to the power of man,
or according to Luke 18:34
to be handed over to the pagans.
>   His real suffering was
>   to live the human life
>   we are living,
>   victims and victimizers
>   of each other,
>   though he was only
>   a victim.
While he was talking
about that human suffering of ours
on that mountain Tabor,
about that suffering in which
he was going to take a new lead,
he started to shine.
First he shone simply like
an African schoolboy,
who rubbed himself from top to bottom
with petroleum jelly;
but then
he shone more and more,
a dazzling light,
full of glory,
while talking.
>   Passion and glory,
>   cross and resurrection,
>   they do not stand next to each other;
>   they grow out of each other.
>   The suffering of Jesus
>   consisted in his desire
>   to be with us

in our hopes and in our struggles
for justice and integrity,
giving himself
to others,
to *all* the others.

17.

THE FRUITLESS FIG TREE

(Luke 13:1–9)

A soldier,
a military commander,
was ruling the country.
His name was Pontius Pilate.
This military dictator
had done something horrible
and blasphemous:
he had killed people in the temple
while they were sacrificing to God.
He had mingled their blood
with the blood
of their sacrificial lambs.
And God,
God had NOT intervened.
God seemed to have approved
because heaven had remained
closed.

 Something else had happened.
 There had been something
 like an earthquake,
 a real "act of God,"

and a tower in town had fallen in,
killing eighteen people
in the rubble.
And people were wondering:
"WHY?"
Why did God allow things like that
to happen?
When we hear those things
we often start to doubt
whether there is any God at all.
>   But that was not the question
>   of the people around Jesus.
>   They had another question.
>   They were not wondering about God;
>   they were wondering
>   about those victims who died.
>   Why did they die?
When Jews
in the time of Jesus
told the story of a disaster,
about a road accident,
a burnt-out house,
an armed robbery,
a flood,
an earthquake,
or something like that,
they were obliged
>   (according to a custom
>   prescribed in the Talmud,
>   a law added to the law)
to finish their story
saying:
"Blessed be God,
who judges rightly."
>   They were not wondering
>   about God;
>   they were wondering
>   about those people killed.

For what hidden crimes
had they been punished?
They were thinking in the old terms
of Job's friends,
those friends who told Job:
"Don't deny it,
you must have been doing something
wrong,
you must have been sinning;
can you remember
a guiltless man,
who perished,
or have you ever seen
good men brought to nothing?"
And many of us,
even today,
reason in the same way.
In a country next to ours,
terrible things had happened:
a bishop was killed;
the blood of Christians
had been spilt.*
Some countries in the United Nations
wanted a commission of investigation,
but other countries,
for all kinds of fishy reasons,
voted against that commission.
During the night of the day
that followed that voting
a lot of the countries
who had voted against the commission
were struck by an earthquake
and thousands died,
and we said:
"You see,
there you are,
justice is done!"

They went to Jesus,
not to find out
about God;
there was no question about God
but about those people who died:
"Why did THEY perish;
what had gone wrong with THEM?"
It had not happened to the people
who went to Jesus;
they had survived;
they had obviously been all right;
why had it happened to those others?
He took up their question,
and he said:
"Do you really think
that the Galileans who suffered like that
were greater sinners than the other Galileans?
Do you really think
that the eighteen that were killed
in the rubble
of that earth tremor
were more guilty
than the others in Jerusalem?
I tell you,
THEY WERE NOT.
NO, but unless YOU repent
you all will perish
as they did."

     And there they stood,
     all of them.
     They had been trying to do
     what we all try to do.
     They had been trying to judge
     the people around them.
     They had been trying to draw a line
     between the just and the unjust,
     between the oppressor and the oppressed,

> between the poor and the rich,
> between the pure and the impure,
> between the bad and the good,
> between those to be punished
> and those to be saved.

And they put themselves,
of course,

> with the just,
> with the oppressed,
> with the poor,
> with the pure,
> with the good,
> with those to be rewarded.

And there they were
standing in front of the man
they had come to see,
because they thought
that he was introduced,
better than any one of them
into the ways of God.

> They had hoped to be confirmed
> by him
> in their righteousness,
> and there they stood
> in their shame.
> And they were very upset
> because he said
> that if they did not convert
> they were all going to perish,
> the whole lot of them,
> cut down like useless trees.

But he saw their fright,
the blood dancing
in front of their eyes,
the houses crumbling on top of their heads,
and he told them a story:
the story about the fruitless fig tree.

One day the father
had come down from heaven
to him, Jesus,
the gardener,
in charge of God's *shamba,*
called WORLD.
And he told them
how he and his father
had been walking around
in that garden,
and how his father had stopped
in front of that fig tree
without any fruits,
how he had stopped in front
of us.
And he told them
how his father had said:
"You have been taking care of this thing
for so many years,
and look at it;
it is still hopeless
and fruitless;
cut it down,
throw it away."
And he told them
how he had answered his father:
"Lord, leave it alone,
this year too,
until I have cleared it up
and manured it;
it may bear fruit
next year;
if not,
then you can cut it down."
And the father let go.
It is in that way
that Jesus warned them;

it is in that way
that Jesus warns us,
that he warns humankind,
that he warns this world;
and it is in that way as well
that he seems to answer
that other question of ours:
Why does God allow all this,
why does he not come back,
why does he not finish the pain?
>   As Saint Peter wrote:
>   "The Lord is not being slow
>   to carry out his promises,
>   as anybody else might be called slow;
>   he is being patient with you all,
>   wanting nobody to be lost,
>   and everybody to be brought
>   to change his ways."
He, the Lord, knows
better than we
what to do.
>   His disciples suggested to him once
>   that he uproot all the evil
>   in the field of this world:
>   "Why are all those weeds spoiling
>   the good grain;
>   do you want us to go
>   and to pull it out?"
He answered:
>   "NO, let both grow,
>   because if you start to weed now
>   you might destroy all."
>   ALL OF US,
>   let us first grow
>   in goodness.

*The bishop killed was the Anglican Archbishop Janani Luwum in Uganda.
See sermon 14 above.

18.

THAT OLDEST SON

(Luke 15:1–3, 11–32)

Famous people are never left alone.
They are always surrounded by others
who want to catch them out.
They sit down
and a bunch of journalists sit
down at the next table.
They stand up to walk away
and they are photographed
from the treetops.
They come out of a car
and microphones are dangling
in front of their mouths,
hoping for
    a provoking,
    a sensational,
    a shocking statement.
And so it was with
Jesus.
They were out, day and night,
to catch him,
they checked him

on his food,
on his healings,
on the times he was healing,
on his tax,
on his bank account,
on his father,
on his mother,
on his ways of transport,
on his clothing,
on how often he washed his hands,
on his creed,
and on his company.
That company was poor:
he sat down with prostitutes,
he did not walk away from that adulterous woman,
he ate with those who exploited the poor
and who collaborated with the oppressors.
He ate, and worse,
he drank with sinners.
Now and then,
and probably very often
he must have been annoyed
and pestered to tears
because of them.
Now and then
he ran away from them.
But sometimes he faced them
directly,
and most times he did this
by telling them a story.
And that is what he did
in the episode
we read
this morning.
They said contemptuously:
"You eat with sinners";
they said contemptuously:
"This man eats with sinners."

They did not even want
to take his name
in their mouths.
 And then he tells them
 that story about those three,
 that father and his two sons,
 about that youngest son,
 who got half the estate
 and who went off to town;
 and he told them
 how he drank
 and went to the casinos
 and bars
 and how he danced and played
 and how he lost all his money.
He told them
how he then
was obliged to herd pigs;
and they all knew
how a Jew herding pigs
was cursed by their law.
He told them
how he ate husks,
pigs' swill,
left over from the kitchen
of the local university;
and they all knew
about their proverb that said:
"If a Jew has to eat pigs' swill,
he will change his mind."
And he told them
that that was what happened.
He changed his mind;
he did not convert,
not at all;
he got hungry,
and he learned his story
by heart:

I will say:
"Father, I have sinned;
give me some food,
please."
And then he told them
how that father,
a stately gentleman,
old and stiff
and full of dignity,
a man who never ran,
a man who was so rich,
that he never needed to run,
how that man,
when he saw his son,
started to run,
and how he embraced him
and kissed him
and how he said,
when he got the smell of those pigs
in his nose:
"Quick, bring out the best robe,"
and how he washed him
and dressed him
and how he ordered
to have the fattened calf killed.
    It was obvious what Jesus meant:
    he wanted to point out
    that he treated sinners
    the way he did
    because of that Father of his.
    And he finished the story by saying:
    "And they began to celebrate."
But something must have happened.
Did they not understand?
Were they still sulking?
Had things not got clear?
Because,

after having finished this story,
he starts again
and tells them a second one.
The one about that oldest son,
who did not come in
and who did not agree.
> That oldest son
> reasoned like the scribes
> and the Pharisees.
> He refused to sit at table
> with his brother: the sinner.
> He wanted to kick him back
> in the gutter of the street,
> where, after all, he had ended up.
> That is where his brother should stay
> to rot.
He came home,
he heard the music,
he smelled the calf over the fire,
he saw the servants running about,
he asked:
"What is going on over here?"
And he was informed about
what had happened,
and he became very angry
and very jealous
and he refused to go in
and join the party.
He refused to sit down
with a sinner,
with that fellow
who had done all the things
he had always wished to do,
but he had never done.
> And the father came out again,
> but this time he did not run.
> And he said to his father:

"That *son of yours,*
that useless one,
that womanizer,
that ex-sugardad,
how could you kill that calf
for him?"
And the father answered,
and he said:
"That *brother of yours*
was dead,
and he has come to life;
he was lost and now
he is found."

The oldest son said:
"that son of yours";
the father said:
"that brother of yours!"
It was that reminder
that did it:
"your brother."
And they both
went in.
Jesus had made his point.
They left him.
And he went on
contacting those brothers and sisters of his,
those brothers and sisters of us,
he went on contacting them and us
because of the reason he had given them.

If he had not taken that attitude,
none of us would ever have been able
to be invited by him.
None of us would ever have been allowed
to sit at a table with him,
because who of us
is
without sin?

19.

SHE IS WE

(John 8:1–11)

Lent has lost quite something
of its sting.
Did you eat less?
Did you eat less well?
Did you drink less?
Did you drink only water?
Did you go out less?
Did you go only to church?
Did you eat fish on Friday?
Could you afford eating fish on Friday?
Was the eating of that expensive fish
a mortification?
     And yet, I think
     that Lent got, in a way,
     a new bite.
     During Lent we are supposed
     to mortify ourselves.
     The greatest mortification
     we can go in for
     is to have a look at ourselves,
     to have a look at humankind

and its doings,
its chances,
and its failures.
And from that point of view
Lent
is getting more and more painful every year.
Most of us grew up
with violence raging around us:
there was a Second World War,
there was over here in Kenya
the emergency,
there was the Vietnamese war,
and even at the moment
we are still surrounded
by violence, degradation,
torture, murder,
and evils like that.
Over the last week,
two presidents and one cardinal
were killed.
Priests were shot,
not to speak about all those
so-called unimportant and nameless ones
who were shot and maimed.
Stones were thrown,
men beat up men,
the same story all over.
People who decided
years ago
that they were not going to the cinema
anymore,
because of all the violence shown in films,
will also have to decide
that they are not going to read any papers
anymore,
that they are not going to listen to the news
anymore,
because of all that violence.

It is hard to think about all this,
it is difficult to speak about it;
it is also, however,
very difficult to escape from it.
Nobody is without sin;
we cannot close our eyes and ears to it.
It makes one wonder,
it makes one wonder,
it makes one wonder,
very much
about others,
but also about ourselves
and about humankind.
In the Gospel of Saint John,
there is
on several occasions
a mysterious woman.
She has no name,
she is anonymous.
In Samaria
she asked for water,
for living water.
Somewhere else
Jesus speaks about that woman
giving birth
in great pain.
And today
that woman without a name
is brought in front of him
accused of adultery.
Who is she,
why is she nameless?
Some specialists have been studying
this issue,
and they say
that she has no name,
because her name really is
HUMANKIND.

That anonymous lady
represents all of us,
the whole of humankind.
I admit that this is mysterious,
I admit that it is a kind of mysticism
that is difficult to follow.
It is too old for us;
we are no longer accustomed to that language
and those ideas of the Bible.
Nevertheless it is a fact
that in the Old Testament
God considers HUMANKIND
as his BRIDE,
as his wife,
as his woman.
And there she is:
asking for water in Samaria,
caught in her sins
in Jerusalem.
And he looks at her,
his bride,
that adulteress,
and he bends down,
and he looks at her again,
playing with his hand in the sand,
and in the end he was alone with her,
and he lets her go,
saying:
"I am not going to condemn you."
And she walks away,
while he adds:
"But do not sin any more;
be faithful."
Afterwards,
that nameless woman,
humankind,
that bride of God,
is mentioned by him again,

as giving birth,
in great pains,
to a new human being,
to a new humankind.
 It is in that rather mysterious light
 that we should see
 what we read in the papers,
 what we hear over the radio,
 what we see in our streets
 and on
 the television;
 it is in that light
 that we are invited
 to see the blood
 and the pain
 all around us.
We are not left,
we are not lost;
something is going to happen,
something is happening.
That is
what Paul also wanted to tell us
in the second reading
of today:
 "I am far from thinking
 that I have already won;
 all I can say is
 that I forget the past
 and strain ahead
 for what is still to come.
 I am racing for the finish,
 for the prize,
 to which God calls us
 UPWARD
 to receive in Jesus Christ."
When that woman
stood before Jesus,
he was her hope.

He did not deceive her,
he did not condemn her;
he told her
that she should not sin any more,
that all the violence
and that all the bloodshed
should stop.
And that she,
on and with his word,
was able to do just that.
He will not deceive us
either,
because
she is we,
she is us.

20.

ECCE HOMO

(Luke 22:14–23:56)

We just heard
the story of the passion
of Our Lord Jesus Christ.
We are accustomed to that story;
it does not do much to us anymore,
we have heard it too often.
We are barred from its
meaning and message.
 We say very easily
 that we should follow him
 in his suffering,
 that we should suffer
 as he suffered.
 And we misunderstand
 its significance.
In Luke's Gospel
Pilate did not want to condemn
Jesus.
He says so three times:
 "I find no case against this man,"
 "I found no case against this man,"
 "I have found no case against this man."

119

But he gives in,
and Mark adds
that he knew
that they had betrayed him
OUT OF ENVY.
And that might indicate
what Pilate intended to say
when he said:
"ECCE HOMO,"
"Look at man!"
    Look at man,
    how spiteful,
    how envious,
    how jealous,
    how hopeless
    he is.
    Look at this man Jesus,
    how he became a play-ball
    of all kinds of passions
    and anger around him;
    look at how they treated
    and betrayed him.
Look at man's fate
and his history.
If we take the words
of Pilate
like that,
we are looking at ourselves
when we are looking at Jesus.
    When we meditate
    upon his suffering,
    when we look at him,
    we are looking at the fate
    of every man and woman,
    the lot of ourselves
    in this world,
    our suffering and
    our death.

We should not suffer
as he suffered;
he suffered
as we suffer.
The pains he took upon himself
are our normal human lot;
it is our normal human condition
in this world of ours
that is not yet
restored in its original goodness
and fulness of life.
>   He showed us
>   how to behave in our passion.
>   He shows us
>   how to understand it.
>   He shows us
>   how it opens a way to fulfilment.
Luke told his passion
in such a way
that his readers
and the church of his time
would be able
to recognize its own suffering
in the passion of Jesus.
>   He makes it very clear
>   that Jesus was not killed
>   by the Romans
>   or because of his political
>   condemnation by Pilate.
>   Jesus was killed
>   by the leaders
>   of a people
>   that followed him weeping
>   and lamenting
>   and that nevertheless
>   had plotted against him.
His suffering was not new;
it is old, it is ours.

Luke puts
three words in his mouth
on the cross:
"Father, forgive them!"
"Father they do not know
what they are doing."
"Father into your hands
I commend my spirit."
He did not show only
how we should suffer;
he also showed us
that we should participate
in human history,
that we should take
the cross of that participation
upon ourselves
not in violence and anger,
but in power and goodness,
as he did,
opening new visions
of justice,
humanity,
and brotherhood.
It is in that suffering
that we should
follow him.

21.

THEY BELIEVED

(John 20:1–9)

The tomb was empty.
The man they had betrayed
and killed
had disappeared.
 Mary of Magdala said:
 "They have stolen him;
 where would they have taken him?"
Peter and John
drew another conclusion;
they said:
"He is risen!"
 They expressed
 in the most radical way
 a belief every human being
 has somewhere:
 the belief that goodness
 and godliness
 will win.
Everything we do
and believe
is colored by that
insight.

In practically every book
and theater play,
western,
or Kung Fu film
that theme comes through.
The good and the just
will win,
and if they don't
we know
that something went wrong;
they should have done so.
It is also
one of the reasons
that so many of us
are interested
in stories about moral courage.
The courage
of a mother who trains
her handicapped child
for years and years,
until that child can stand upright
and speak.
    The courage of the man
    who lost his hands and his feet,
    but who learned how to write
    and paint
    with his mouth.
At Easter,
when believing in Christ's resurrection,
we express
that general belief
in its extreme form.
We believe that
goodness and
godliness
won in this world
and will win in the time
to come.

This belief
also includes
some moral consequences
for us:
we are going to win
and not going to be buried,
and not going to slip into nothingness,
insofar as we are on
his side,
the side of that goodness,
the side of the life
that did not die,
though he seemed to be buried
in that tomb,
for three days.

22.

THOMAS'S RISK

(John 20:24–29)

There seems to be something
strange
about Thomas.
He does not seem to be willing
to believe.
He does not want
to hear.
He does not want to believe
that resurrection at all.
　　Why not?
　　Why did it disturb him?
　　Why was he not glad,
　　just like all the others?
　　Why did he look for an excuse,
　　for a justification,
　　for his unbelief?
He was like that heavy smoker,
a very heavy one,
who hears from his doctor
that the way he is smoking
is a health hazard,

that it is definitely NOT
the way to success,
but to a terminal disease.
He should stop.
He should stop forthwith.
But he does not want
to accept this.
He does not want
to believe it,
so he looks for all kinds of reasons
to be able to continue
smoking.
He says:
    "But that doctor
    smokes himself."
He says:
    "Driving in modern traffic
    is a health hazard too,
    but you don't expect me
    to stay at home
    because of that,
    do you?"
He says:
    "Smoking is bad for people
    with a weak constitution,
    but in my family
    we have strong constitutions;
    my father smoked more than I do,
    and he died at the age of ninety-two
    while smoking."
Why did Thomas not believe?
What was his difficulty?
The story itself
explains his problem.
He wanted to see the wounds,
he wanted to see the signs
of the suffering,
he wanted to see the scars:

he could not believe,
because he did not want to believe,
that that suffering had led
to glory.
He could not believe,
because *he did not want*
to believe it.
And he did not want to believe it
because of the unavoidable consequences
of that belief.
Let us not forget
that he was out
that Easter night.
He had given up.
He had gone home.
He blamed himself
for ever having believed
that the Jesus' type of life
would bring him anywhere.
He sat down with his friends,
his old friends,
his "before Christ" friends,
and they told him:
"Didn't we tell you
that it would be no good?
Nobody can overcome the corruption
of this world,
not Jesus either.
Here,
take a glass of beer,
forget about it.
Let us not exaggerate,
let us live our normal destiny,
let us be realistic!"
And in a way
he,
Thomas,
was glad
that it was all over.

After all,
living with Christ
and like Jesus
meant a terrific extra trouble;
you had to walk
on your toes
the whole "blessed" day.
He did not want to start
that
all over again.
      He was afraid,
      really afraid,
      that the resurrection story
      might be true.
      And he was not the only one
      in that fear.
If you read the resurrection stories
in the Gospels carefully,
you will notice
that most of the disciples
had that fear.
Those stories and reports say:
      nineteen times that they were afraid
      and upset,
      seventeen times that they were doubting
      and unbelieving,
      and only four times
      that they were
      full of joy.
      Mark never mentions
      that joy at all,
      but Mark does mention
      their fear five times
      and their doubts
      four times.
Thomas wanted to see the wounds
that led to glory.
He hoped that they
would not be there,

because if they were not there,
he would not have to change his life
either.
>   But they were there;
>   he saw them,
>   himself,
>   he felt them,
>   himself,
>   he drew the conclusion
>   himself,
>   and he left
>   for his endless
>   mission journeys,
>   to be killed like
>   all the others
>   with the exception of John,
>   who died in exile.
Do we dare believe?
Are we really willing to believe
that Jesus' type of life
leads to glory?
>   Aren't we, maybe,
>   too much like Thomas
>   that night,
>   those eight days?
>   Not wanting to believe
>   because of the consequences.
The consequences
that WE have to live,
the actions and the passions
of Jesus Christ
at peril
of being judged by him
as not having lived
at all.

23.

DO YOU LOVE ME?

(John 21:12–20)

They had their mouths full of fish,
his fish;
he had caught it for them,
he had fried it for them,
and he had asked:
"Do you like it?"
and they had answered:
    "Yes,
    definitely yes."
    And they patted
    their filled stomachs
    with that very nice glow
    of being satisfied inside,
    and they said
    once more:
    "Yes,
    we like that fish."
They had their hands full of bread,
his bread;
he had baked it for them,
or he had bought it for them.

He asked:
"Do you like it?"
And they looked at it,
and they put it in their mouths,
and while they were chewing it,
carefully,
to be sure of the taste,
they said:
    "Yes,
       definitely yes.
       It is exactly as bread
       should be,
       so early in the morning."
       And they looked at him
       very happily.
And then he asked them
that other question,
a very old question,
a very human question,
a very tricky question,
a very ambiguous question,
a very deceiving question:
    "Do you love me,
       Peter,
       do you love me?"
Every time a man asks a woman
that question:
"Do you love me?"
and she answers:
"Yes, I love you!"
What does she mean?
Every time a girl asks a man
that question:
"Do you love me?"
and he answers:
"Yes, I love you!"
What does he mean?

Does he mean that he likes
to have *his* eyes filled with her;
does he mean that he likes
to have *his* hands full of her;
does he mean that he likes
to have *his* satisfaction with her,
or is he really speaking,
when answering that question—
"Do you love ME"—
about *her*?
Peter said:
"Yes, sir, I love you."
That is all he said,
and the question Jesus asked
had not been answered,
at least not in a
clear way.
    Peter might have meant:
    "I love you,
    because *I* love to be with you,
    because *I* love to eat your fish,
    because *I* love your bread so much,
    because *I* love myself."
So Jesus asked him
a second time:
"Do you love me?"
And again Peter did not really
answer his question.
Again he said:
"Yes, I love you,"
without making it clear
what he really meant.
So Jesus asked him
a third time:
"Do you love me?"
And when Peter,
again,

did not answer the question,
Jesus answered it
himself,
and he said:
>"If you really love ME,
>if you really love MY approach,
>if you really love MY style of life,
>if you really love MY way,
>then
>be interested
>not in yourself,
>but in others."

Brothers and sisters,
we are living in a community
where we are blaming
each other,
very often,
very much.
And is it not true
to say
that we blame each other
almost always
for the same thing?
>"Everybody seems to care only
>for himself
>or for herself."

I do not say
that that is the picture,
the total picture,
of this university.
It is not.
Every student who gets
into trouble
in this University of Nairobi
is
surrounded by friends,
and I never saw it differently.

And yet,
we blame each other,
for so much carelessness,
for so much selfishness,
in all kinds of things,
in the refectory,
in the classroom,
in the library,
in the halls,
lack of care,
lack of interest,
lack of love.

    So many of us say
    that we love Jesus.
    So many of us come together
    to witness to this;
    so many come together
    to sing it,
    and nevertheless . . .

There remains that question of Jesus:
"Do you love ME?"
That is our vocation,
that is the human vocation.
It is a vocation
and call
that is so bitterly necessary
in this world of ours,
in the world of these days.
It is a vocation and a call
that we should take upon ourselves
as a community;
it is a vocation
that is asking for leaders,
for all kinds of leaders,
    for doctors,
    for lawyers,
    for journalists,

and teachers,
but also for people
specialized in religious leadership,
like those apostles of his,
for priests,
for dedicated people.
Let us pray . . .

24.

THEY WILL NEVER GET LOST

(John 10:27–30)

About forty years ago,
when this world was a very different place,
I was a small
and, according to the photos of that time,
a very thin boy.
I was a mass-server
and a choirboy,
and one day we had an outing.
We went to a forest
with a kind of pond in the middle,
and while playing in that pond,
I suddenly fell from a tree trunk
on which I was sitting
and I fell in the water.
I bumped my head
and because of my fright,
I forgot to swim.
  I went under once,
   and I saw all kinds of bubbles,

and I came up
and went under for a second time,
again seeing all kinds of bubbles.
I came up,
and just when I was disappearing
for the third time
the curate who was with us
came running along.
He jumped in the water
and he dragged me out.
I was unconscious
and everybody thought I was dead.
But after quite some minutes,
I came back.
And suddenly
I was a hero.
One of my aunts even did
a thing she had never done before.
She invited me for tea,
and when I had got my tea,
she asked me:
"What happened while you were drowning,
what did you see?"
I told her that I saw
only water and air bubbles,
and she was disappointed.
She asked me
whether I had said
an act of contrition,
and I told her
that I forgot.
    And then she told me
    that people in those moments
    that they are going to die
    see all kinds of things,
    that they see their whole lives
    in a kind of short film,
    and that there is a light
    and . . .

What happens during and after
our death?
Saint John gives us his answer today,
and so does Jesus.
They say
that God will spread his tent over us;
they say
that we will never thirst or hunger again;
they say
that the sun will not burn us
and that the wind will do us no harm;
they say
that we will never get lost,
that we will never be rustled
or stolen.
     In other words:
     we will be understood,
     we will be received,
     we will be welcomed,
     we will be taken up,
     WE,
     not only YOU and ME,
     but WE
     will be taken up
     by HIM.
At the moment
there are very many confirmations
of what my aunt had heard,
about that quick film
and about that light
that people experience
while dying.
Many people "died,"
you know,
and came back.
There are some in the Gospel,
Lazarus,
that boy from Naim,
that daughter of a Roman official.

But even nowadays
this happens so often
that recently a study was made
of 150 cases.
    And in all the reports
    of those people who came back,
    people who did not know
    of each others' stories,
    you find more or less
    the same ingredients:
        they tell how they left their bodies,
        how they saw their bodies
        outside themselves,
        how they, then, went through
        something like a dark tunnel,
        and how there was something like
        a growing light,
        something like the sun,
        but it did not blind or burn,
        and they saw, indeed,
        in short flashes
        their whole lives,
        the good and the bad,
        and then the light proved to be
        something personal,
        a somebody.
        And they report
        how that somebody
        looked at those life-flashes
        too,
        and how all was understood by him
        and how he approved the selfless acts
        and how he disapproved of the selfish ones
        but how he even saw
        those reproachable acts
        as part of a learning process.
        And after that . . .
        they came back,
        changed people.

They all said
that the light
    —some call it Christ,
    some call it God,
    some call it Light—
was kind and protective,
humorous and understanding,
forgiving and fulfilling.
    We do not need those reports
    to know all that.
    The Gospels tell us
    all there is to know:
    the shelter will be there,
    sun, wind, and rain will do no harm
    to us anymore.
    The tears will not only be wiped away;
    there will be no tears anymore.
    The Light will be there
    and all whom we love
    now,
    but the others
    whom we don't love so much
    now,
    will be there
    too,
    but changed,
    just as we will be there,
    changed.

25.

EVERYONE SHOULD KNOW

(John 13:31–35)

Some time ago
the Department of Philosophy and Religious Studies
organized a theological forum,
and for a whole week
Education Auditorium 2
was filled with hundreds of students
every evening
to listen to talks on
the modern criticism of religion
and the answers to that criticism.
    One evening,
    one of the speakers
    said that Christianity
    was useless
    in the struggle for a new earth,
    because,
    he said,
    it preaches a shortcut
    out of our human problems,
    a shortcut
    that always seems to cause a short-circuit,
    and a power failure.

That shortcut was,
according to him,
that text of the Gospel of today:
"LOVE ONE ANOTHER."
He said that this saying was
    so wide,
    so impractical,
    so abstract,
    so much in the air,
    and therefore so mystifying
    and diverting from the real problems
    that it did not help a soul.
He wanted a much more practical
and concrete approach,
something dialectical,
he said,
in view of the reconstruction of the world
everybody seems to think about
nowadays.
    He doubted the validity of charity
    and especially of Christian charity.
    He doubted its validity
    because he doubted its efficacy.
And let us be honest about it;
he had some very good reasons
to think so.
    We are supposed
    to love one another
    in this world,
    in this country,
    on this campus,
    in such a way,
    that people will say of us:
    "Look how they love
    each other;
    look how they love the others;
    they must be disciples of that man
    Jesus Christ,

who gave his life
in the way they are doing
that."
We must love one another
in such a way
that the new earth
John spoke about
in the second reading of today,
that the new city of humankind
and the new city of God and humanity
grow among us.
Kenya is one of the most Christian countries
in Africa.
Its Christianity is young
and very enthusiastic.
It is visible everywhere.
I never saw a country
in which that Christianity
is more visible in the streets
on a Sunday-morning:
preachers and processions,
healings and the gift of tongues
everywhere.
Kenya is a country that teems
with preachers and prophets,
indigenous ones and imported ones.
They all preach the knowledge of God,
they all preach brotherhood and love,
but they all,
indeed,
seem to be very abstract,
very inefficient,
very a-historical,
very un-engaged,
and very undialectical
in that preaching.
Jesus did not preach like that;
he did not speak in that way,

he did not come in that way,
he did not act in that way,
he did not live in that way.
> He spoke a human language,
> he spoke a concrete language
> in a concrete context.
> That context was so concrete
> that he was arrested
> and killed
> in the name of all the upholders
> of the old law and order
> he had come to change.

He formed a community
that went out preaching
and healing,
a community
that organized assistance and help
to widows and orphans,
to the sick and the drop-outs.
They organized a better way of life,
a new earth,
a new world,
within the concrete context
of their world.
> The final test for our belief in Jesus,
> and that means for us as well,
> the final test for our belief in God,
> is not the knowing of our creed,
> the beauty of our talk,
> but our concrete love
> for human beings,
> for each other.
> > And we need that love.
> > We need to love.
> > We need to be loved.

26.

WE AND THE SPIRIT

(John 14:23–29)

According to the Gospel of today,
a Spirit will be sent,
a Spirit that is going to renew
the whole of the world.
And that means of course
nothing but
the whole of humankind.
    In the second reading of today,
    that Spirit is present,
    because the disciples of Jesus Christ
    write almost triumphantly
    after one of the meetings they had:
    "The Spirit and we ourselves
    have decided."
The new Spirit was there,
the new Spirit is here,
but that Spirit was sent into a world
that was
and is
still old,
into a world that has to be renewed,
into a world that has to be developed.

A man responsible
for the religious education
in one of the larger schools
of this republic Kenya
wrote a letter
this week
to the Panel of the Kenyan Institute
of Education,
in charge of the religious syllabus
in Kenya.
He wrote:
When the students come to school,
they are all very enthusiastic
about their Christianity.
They come to the Sunday services,
they discuss all kinds of issues;
very lively,
they are full of expectations,
they are full of hope,
they are looking for the poor,
and they try very hard to live up
to their ideals.
And as if the new world has started
already,
they call each other
brother and sister
and God their father.
But when they reach the higher forms
they slip
or fall away.
When you ask them
why,
they will tell you
that they started to understand
how hard,
how political,
how cruel,
how businesslike
this world is

full of deceit,
full of bribery,
full of threat,
full of fight.
They will tell you
how they started to understand
that Christians who live up to their ideals
have no chance of surviving,
that Christians are not adapted
to that type of life
and how in the struggle for survival
they will be eaten by
the hyenas,
the vultures,
the wild dogs,
and the rats.
And as those students
do not want to be pretenders
or hypocrites
as so many Christians
are in this world,
as they would not like
to give the wrong impression
about their hope,
Jesus Christ,
they prefer in all honesty
to opt out in time,
calling themselves
victims of their
"realism."
Though invited to a new life,
they choose the old one.
But the world and humankind
will NEVER change
and never come one step further
in this way.
Though it is still unusual,
it is nevertheless possible
to see the person of Jesus,

his life and his death,
as a new step forward,
a new evolutionary step forward
in God's creative history.
In the beginning matter developed
slowly, slowly, slowly,
under the influence of God's creative power
into life.
That was quite something,
a mutation,
a change-over,
a jump.
    And then under that same power of God,
    slowly, slowly, slowly,
    life developed in all kinds of directions,
    and one of those directions
    was humankind,
    and that again was
    quite a change,
    a mutation,
    a tremendous changeover,
    a jump.
And then in the fullness of time
God introduced to us
his son Jesus Christ,
a completely new version of humankind,
a new creature,
a new creation,
a person totally new,
of a different Spirit,
with new possibilities,
with a new type of love,
with a new life-code,
an enormous change,
a new jump,
a new person.
    According to that teacher,
    here somewhere in Kenya,
    his students know that but too well.

They realize that Jesus
is a jump
and brings that newness,
but they say:
  "WE can't do it,
  the world is not ready for him."
  And they hesitate,
  or they refuse,
  as so many hesitated
  or refused before,
  leaving the world and humankind
  as it is,
  and as it was,
  and as it has been
  for so very, very long.
Let us pray
that we may be willing
to receive,
to accept,
and to stick
to the Spirit of God.

27.

OFF HE WAS

(Acts 1:1–11)

There they were standing,
chatting jovially
together with him
about the kingdom to come,
about the world to end.
He was in the center,
they stood around,
John nearest,
Peter surest.
    And suddenly
his feet left the ground;
he started to go up,
smoothly but surely,
higher and higher,
higher and higher,
higher and higher,
until they could hardly see him any more,
a small dot
against the immense sky.
They strained their eyes
and then decided that they could not see him
anymore.

OFF he was.
OFF he was,
the Savior of this world.
He flew out of it,
leaving it seemingly
as it had been before,
because when they went home,
after his dramatic and spectacular exit,
there were still the normal police-checks
by the Roman occupational forces
on Temple Road;
there were the sick and the crippled,
there were the rich and the poor,
there were the ignorant and the illuminated,
the destitutes,
the pickpockets,
the deceived girls,
and the endless political intrigues.
But off he was.
Before he went
he had told them
that it would be best for them
that he go away,
because, he said:
"If I do not go,
you would never be able to receive the Spirit
yourselves;
you would never be willing to acknowledge
that Spirit in you,
you would always remain looking at me,
you would not take up any responsibility,
you would gape at me."
And that is what they were doing,
even after his disappearance.
They remained staring up,
with open mouths
and watering eyes.
Angels had to come down
to tell them to move on,

to get out of the place,
to do what he had told them to do.
And dazed they stumbled back,
from the mountain to Jerusalem,
now and then still looking over their shoulders
to check once more.
They went to a room,
they locked the door,
they closed the shutters,
they slammed the bolts,
they put a piece of chewing gum in the keyhole,
and they put a table against the door.
    They tried to pray;
    did they really try to pray?
    Now and then somebody would check
    what was happening outside.
    Was the end near or nearer?
But nothing was happening outside,
everything went on as normal,
the good and the bad,
just as before.
    John said:
    "I met him at the tenth hour,
    I accepted him immediately
    as my personal savior,
    he loved me very much,
    I was allowed to sit next to him at the last supper,
    he let me put my head against his chest."
    But what did that help the world?
    What did it help John?
    He was off!
Peter said:
"He really trusted me,
he prayed especially for me, he said,
he made me the boss,
didn't he?"
The boss of what?
He was off.
What was left?

Nobody left this world ever
so thoroughly.
He did not leave
a single bone or tooth
in this world,
nothing at all.
All the others had their own stories
in that upper room,
Philip and James,
Thomas,
and even the specialist in hopeless cases,
Jude.
But what did those stories help?
And then, the tenth day, it happened,
heaven opened,
a storm was heard,
fire appeared,
he came back to them.
His Spirit descended into them,
and there was fire and lightning,
enthusiasm and little flames,
sparks all over the place.
And then they suddenly understood.
What had gripped him,
gripped them,
and the table was pushed away
from the door,
and the door was opened
(they must have had some difficulties
with that piece of chewing gum in the keyhole)
and they started.
They started to do what?
They started to do what *he did;*
they started to try to save the world.
They were not trying to save
themselves,
but the world.
They were not interested in their salvation
so much;

they were interested in the salvation
of humankind.
They did not judge the world,
as most ecclesiastical leaders are fond
of doing,
they were like Jesus who had said:
"I did not come to judge the world,
nor to condemn it;
I came to rescue it."
They did not start a new political party;
they started to do something much more fundamental;
they started to try to introduce
a new set of values
and principles.
Politics do not seem
to help much in this world,
exactly because something much more fundamental
seems to be missing in this world.
And it is there
that Jesus
and his disciples
found their field of struggle,
a struggle that continues,
combating the evil,
the greed, the pride, the complacency,
the thick skins and the fat bellies,
bribery and dishonesty,
unchecked lust, brotherization,*
profiteering,
and all those other things
that make this world
and its people
stink
and
rot.
Christians have always had the tendency
to try to be with their Lord in heaven.
They remain staring up,
open-mouthed,

pie-in-the-sky adorers,
sanctuary dwellers,
liturgy revellers.

> We should be with Jesus,
> we should be with the Spirit,
> combating evil,
> changing the world,
> changing ourselves,
> changing its values,
> making it more and more
> into what we manage to do
> during this service:
> eating and sharing together.
> It is only on the basis of such
> an ethical change,
> it is only on that type of
> conversion
> that salvation can be built.

*Brotherization: a word used to describe tribal nepotism.

28.

WHY STEPHEN HAD TO DISAPPEAR

(Acts 7:55–60)

The story is about Stephen.
He had been arrested,
and standing before court
he said
that he saw heaven open
and Jesus standing at the right hand
of God the Father.
And when they heard that
the people in court
covered their ears
like small children
who do not want to hear
an unpleasant remark.
    They jumped up,
    they dragged him out of the hall
      (all procedure
      and ceremonial
      were forgotten).

157

They pushed and pulled him
through the streets
to a field outside town,
and there they took off their jackets;
they spat in their hands
and on their chests,
and they stoned him
while he said aloud
and full of compassion:
"Forgive them."

A very obvious case of a conflict,
and a fight
ending in a vulgar lynching party.
Why did they want to do
away with him?
Why did he not fit into
their pattern?
Why had he to be done away with?

The answer seems to be:
because he believed in Jesus.
But what is so wrong with believing
in Jesus Christ?
What is the harm done?
We all believe in him,
and no harm is done
to us!

We do not know so very much
about Stephen.
We know that he was a deacon;
that meant that he was in charge
of helping refugees
and distributing goods to the poor.
We know that he served at table,
that he was full of faith
and the Holy Spirit,
and we know that he worked
miracles.

Those four—
    Spirit,
    faith,
    services,
    and miracles—
    hang together.
If you are full with the Spirit
of Christ, you will be full of Christ.
And one of the most striking things
about Jesus is
his compassion.
Again and again the Gospels
say of him
that he was sorry for
    the poor,
    the sick,
    the oppressed,
    the children,
    the widows,
    the crowds.
All the time he is saying:
    "Don't weep,
    don't worry,
    don't cry,
    don't be afraid."
He speaks about the compassion
    of the good Samaritan,
    of the father
    of the prodigal son.
He is moved to tears,
when thinking
about the disasters
that are going to hit
Jerusalem.
    All his miracles,
    all his teachings,
    all his healings,

his whole life in fact,
his coming and
his going
were based
on that compassion
for us.
Stephen was full of
that same Holy Spirit.
Stephen's faith
was nothing but
a participation
in Christ's compassion,
and that is why he served
and worked miracles.

But why was he killed?
What is wrong with that faith?
What is wrong with that Spirit?
What is wrong with serving?
What is wrong with miracles?
What is wrong with compassion?
I know a person
over here in town
who some years ago,
like Stephen,
functioned like a kind
of deaconess.
She was not officially appointed,
no bishop had consecrated her,
but her community had put her in charge
of the same type of things
that Stephen was in charge of.
She distributed goods,
she helped the poor,
she served at table,
she did her work,
she cooked food,
she worked miracles,

and she was so full of the Holy Spirit
that she believed
that eventually
the whole world would change.
But while doing all this
—she told me herself—
she also started to see
how this world works,
the people around her,
the institutions,
the politicians,
the shopkeepers,
the workers,
the sponsors and the donors,
the rich and the poor.
     And she said
     that one day
     she knelt down
     for the last time,
     and she gave up.
     She switched over completely,
     and she said:
     "I am going to think
     only of myself
     just as all the others do."
     She wanted to be
     like the world
     that she and we live in.
     Her compassion gave in.
     She joined—and she knew very well
     what she was doing—
     the others,
     the world:
a world that does not know him,
a world that does not have his Spirit,
a world that has no compassion,
a world that builds arms,

a world that tortures,
a world that oppresses,
a world that exploits,
a world that is an enemy,
a real enemy of human life,
a world that thinks in terms
of power, money, and prestige,
a world that says with a broad smile:
"Let us develop the neutron bomb;
its advantage is
that it kills *human life*
and that it leaves
the things standing."

> Are you willing
> to live the life of the Spirit
> as Stephen did?
> Are you willing to be
> with his compassion,
> the compassion
> of Jesus Christ
> and of God the Father,
> the Almighty?

If the world would be willing
to live that life
it would change,
and every catastrophe
would be slowly but surely
less and less of a threat.
But it would also mean
that the world as we know it now
would disappear.

> The world around Stephen
> knew this,
> and they did not want this,
> and that is why they took stones
> and murdered him.
> That is why he had to
> disappear.

And yet
their battle was lost.
Even Saul, who took care
of the jackets they had taken off
to be free with their hands,
changed his name
some months afterwards
from Saul to Paul.
The battle is lost.
Stephen won.

29.

PENTECOST, THAT IS, THE FIFTIETH DAY

(John 20:19–23)

The fiftieth day
after the resurrection
the apostles met.
They had been waiting
for all those days
and nothing much had happened
to them.
> They had seen him,
> they had touched him,
> they had seen him again,
> they had seen him leaving,
> they had been sent to Jerusalem
> by a couple of angels,
> but to them
> THEMSELVES
> nothing had happened.
They had decided,
and they had it maybe even
formulated as a kind of ultimatum,

that if nothing happened within
fifty days
they would forget about it.
>They hoped that something
>would happen,
>but they also hoped
>that nothing would happen.
>From that point of view
>they were at the same time
>conservatives
>—let nothing happen—
>and progressives
>—let something,
>let all change.
They were mainly afraid,
they were scared,
they did not like it,
and yet they knew
that something was going to happen.
>He, Jesus,
>had told them
>that he was going to send them
>*a helper,*
>so they would have to DO things,
>and they were not too sure
>that they liked the idea.
>He had told them
>that he was going to send them
>*a consoler,*
>which obviously meant
>that they were going to suffer,
>because only one who suffers
>needs consolers and consolation;
>they were not too eager
>to suffer either.
>He had told them
>that he was going to send them
>*a lawyer, an advocate;*

but you need people like that
only when you are in trouble,
and they were not too sure
that they wanted to be in trouble.
He had spoken about light,
he had spoken about fire,
he had been speaking about doing
greater things than
he had done,
about moving mountains,
about being led
where they would not like to be led,
about going out to all nations,
about going to the ends of the earth,
about appearing before kings and judges,
about arrests and persecutions,
about breaking your bread
and sharing your cup,
about laying down your life
for your friends,
and things like that,
        and,
        to tell the full truth,
        when they thought about it,
        they did not like it.
        And the more they thought about it,
        the less they liked it.
They hoped,
I think,
that that fiftieth day would pass
without any extra fuss,
without any further opening of heaven
or things like that.
        But they did meet;
        they kept to their appointment.
        First it had been decided to meet
        in the evening,
        but they had all been so nervous
        about it,

that they were already there
in the morning,
like a student whose exam starts at nine
but who is already at the exam room,
or near it,
behind a bush,
not to be seen,
at 6 A.M.
There they were
discussing
their ultimatum,
asking each other:
"What are you going to do
if nothing happens?"
telling each other bravely
that even if nothing happened
anymore,
they nevertheless
did not regret
the time they had been
with Jesus.
But suddenly
it did happen:
heaven did open,
there was
noise,
fire,
a large flame,
that divided over smaller ones,
and those smaller flames
set over their heads,
one flame per head;
they stayed on top of those heads
for a second or so,
and they disappeared
into those heads.
And then the thing they had been
most afraid of
took place:

they became enthusiastic,
the little flames exploded in their heads,
and they started to speak in tongues,
and they started to speak in foreign languages,
and they felt uplifted
and HIS SPIRIT was in THEM.
A tremendous experience;
and they suddenly understood
what he had meant:
with his light,
with his fire,
with his spirit,
with his water,
with his salt,
with his ferment,
with his hope,
and with his love.
They all reacted differently,
and yet they all reacted as
ONE.
They all spoke different languages,
and yet they all had
the same message.
All this was only
the innocent beginning,
because that Spirit
forced them out,
and after two thousand years
they reached you and me
and Jesus' Spirit
came with them.
We are here this morning
also
in a room;
we too have been waiting,
seven times seven times,
endlessly;
we too are impatient:

if nothing is going to happen
very soon,
we are going to give up;
we too
are progressive and
conservative at the same time,
    because if anything like his Spirit
    invades us,
    what is going to happen to us?
    We might start speaking languages,
    but in languages you speak only words.
    Just imagine
    if we became like him,
    if we had to break our bread
    and to share our cup,
    as he did.
    Just
    think
    of it.

30.

TRINITY SUNDAY: WE ARE NOT ALONE

(John 16:12–15)

Today is Trinity Sunday.
We commemorate the fact
that God
though alone,
because God is only one,
is not alone,
because he is in three.
That is very difficult to explain;
in fact I would not be able to explain it,
because we really do not know
that much about God;
we only know about ourselves,
about you and me
     There is one thing I know
     about myself
     and also
     about you—
     that nobody likes to be
     completely alone:

170

to eat alone,
to sleep alone,
to walk alone,
to work alone,
to talk alone;
that means to talk
to yourself alone.
To be alone,
totally alone?
It is impossible,
the thought
alone
is unbearable.
Some days ago
I read a story
about a man
who was so alone and lonely
that nobody ever shook his hands,
nobody ever patted his shoulders,
nobody ever gave him a friendly push in his ribs,
nobody ever touched him,
and he felt so lonely,
that he spent his last money
not on some food;
food would not help;
it does not make contact
when you eat it alone.
He did not spend it on a bed;
a bed does not help either.
He did not spend it on a drink;
a drink alone is poison.
He spent his last money
on a hairdresser,
to be touched
and to be taken care of
by someone
for some minutes.

Loneliness
is one of the most frightening experiences
in life.
Did you ever loose your way
in a forest?
Have you ever been so lost
that you did not hear any human voice
anymore,
and no dog barked,
and no truck passed,
and you were totally alone?
Have you ever been alone
in a prison cell,
alone
for some hours,
for twenty-four hours,
for forty-eight hours,
locked up,
and you started to wonder
whether they had not forgotten you,
and you had not even been allowed
to warn anybody at home?
     If you are alone,
     you change completely,
     you dry up,
     you hear noises
     outside and inside
     yourself:
     bubbling noises,
     getting louder and louder;
     it is no good,
     no good.
It is terrible to be alone,
terrible,
even if you are with others.
I heard a report
on a prison
in these, our days.

The prisoners
were rather well taken care of
foodwise,
but they were not allowed to speak.
They were not allowed to work,
and even working together creates contact.
They had to sit,
not against the wall,
but a few yards from the wall
on the floor,
and they were not allowed
to have any contact with the others
at all.
They were not even allowed
to move:
terrible.
     But, you might say,
     does not everybody
     over here at the university
     want a single room?
     A room alone?
     I don't think
     that everybody wants that,
     and those who want
     such a single room,
     do they want that
     to be alone?
Nobody wants to be alone,
and I hope and pray
that none of us
will ever be alone,
imprisoned or lost,
during our lives,
     that none of us
     will ever feel alone,
     between the two walls
     that limit our existence
     over here:

that wall behind us,
the womb of our mother,
out of which we were born,
and that wall before us,
the womb of the earth,
in which we once
are all,
in one way or another,
going to be buried.

One of those two wombs
belongs to the past,
the one of our mother.
One of those two wombs
belongs to our future,
the one of the earth.
Will we be alone
then
while in that earth?

That fellow student of ours,
that friend Richard Amolo,
who died this week
on this campus
and who was buried from this chapel,
is he alone
now,
completely alone,
in a world without hope,
in a world without fellow beings,
in a world without God?

During his requiem mass
the following text
from Saint Paul
was read:

"We want you not to remain
in ignorance, brothers,
about those who sleep in death.
You should not grieve
like the rest of men,
who have no hope;

we believe that Jesus died and rose again,
and so it will be
for those who died.
God will bring them to life,
God will be there
at the other side
of that womb
in the earth."
And God will not only be there;
mere presence is no help,
mere presence does not take
loneliness away;
he will be there to relate to us
    as a father, a parent,
    as a brother, a friend,
    as a loving Spirit.
And that is what we celebrate
today:
God is not alone;
but we are not alone either,
and we will never be.

31.

TO COMMEMORATE
WHAT?

(1 Cor. 11:23–26)

During his last dinner
with his disciples,
Jesus took bread,
he thanked his Father,
he broke the bread,
and he said:
    "This is my body."
And he offered it
to those present.
He then
took the cup,
and he said:
    "This is the cup of my blood,
    that is going to be shed for you,
    for the forgiveness of sins."
And he passed the cup around
and he added:
    "Do this
    to commemorate
    me."

In those last words
he expressed a mission,
an assignment, a task.
> I think that very many of us,
> and rightly so,
> think that the assignment is
> to commemorate that last supper
> by repeating it,
> in order to remember him,
> just as we are doing
> at this very moment
> during this Mass.

That is true,
but it is not
all the truth.
> Did he want to leave us with
> a ritual,
> a rite,
> a commemoration
> in that sense?
> Did he want to leave us with
> a kind of repeated anniversary
> of that last supper
> and of his death?
> Did he want to leave us with
> a priest saying a text
> and us assisting
> at the saying of that text,
> with or without a booklet
> to check that priest?

It is not
all the truth;
there seems to be
more to it.
> When Jesus took his bread
> and that cup,
> when he broke it
> and handed it around,
> he INTERPRETED his death;

that is clear,
because he himself said so:
 "This blood is going to be shed
 in order to redeem,
 in order to liberate."
He saw his death
in the light, or maybe the dark,
of the cross,
but his cross should be seen
in the light and the dark
of his life,
in the light and the dark
of the homework
his Father gave him
before he entered this world
of ours.
His cross was the crown
on his work
during his life.
 He put the shedding of his blood
 in that life-context
 when he tried to explain
 to his compatriots at Nazareth
 what he really wanted to accomplish:
  "He sent me to preach the good news,
  he sent me to free prisoners,
  to make the blind see
  and the deaf hear."
 He put the shedding of his blood
 in that life-context
 when he tried to explain
 to his cousin John
 that he really was the savior to come:
  "Go and tell him
  the blind see,
  the paralyzed walk,
  the lepers have a smooth skin,
  the deaf hear,

the dead are walking again,
and this good message is even given
to the poorest."
When he told his disciples,
do THIS to commemorate me,
that word THIS
did not refer only
to the taking of a piece of bread
or a cup of wine;
it referred also
to the taking up of his
type of life
and his
type of death.

> The sacrament of the Last Supper
> is connected with the bringing
> of new life,
> with the healing of bodies and souls,
> with the restoration of broken
> human relations,
> with the elimination of social
> injustice and inequality,
> with the working at peace
> for all people.

That is our task;
we cannot do that alone,
and that is why this bread
was broken by him,
not among the few
but among the many;
that is why his cup
is passed around
among the many.

> Every man or woman
> who ever tried to solve
> a social problem
> knows that no social problem
> can be solved by one alone.

We need the community,
we need a group,
we need a team;
he too
needed that team,
and that is why
he called us
together
over here
today.

32.

TO LOSE ONE'S LIFE

(Luke 9:18–24)

For most of you
over here in this chapel
this is your last Sunday on the campus,
and for quite some among you
it will be your very last Sunday
over here.
> You are going to leave,
> you are going to enter the world,
> or as one of you told me,
> rather sarcastically:
> "One week more
> and I move from the animal orphanage
> into the national park
> where you tear each other apart
> under supervision."
A new life will start;
some of you would most probably
like to delay a bit longer;
some will postpone;
they will tarmack,*
sit or hang around.

It is not always easy to switch over;
you have to lose a life
to gain a new one.
It is not easy
to pack up and go.
But it is no good
to delay either;
there comes an end to everything.
Every baby once suckles the breast
of its mother for the last time,
and every embrace
breaks up
once.
At least it should,
and that is why the Gospel of today
says:
we have to grow,
we have to shoulder responsibilities,
we have to develop,
we have to increase,
we have to march on,
    the old skin is no longer any good,
    the cocoon too narrow,
    the campus too small,
    the real struggle starts
    for everyone.
But what struggle are you going to join?
Is it going to be your exclusive fight
for a wife,
    a beautiful one;
for a husband,
    a beautiful one;
for a car,
    a big one;
for a position,
    an influential one;
for a house,
    a five-bedroom one;

for a farm,
    an eight-thousand-acre one;
for a scholarship,
    abroad,
      ONLY?
A struggle
in which you fight like mad
to get your part,
and the largest possible one, of
    the zebra skin,
    the elephant tusk,
    and the rhino horn?
Or is it that other struggle,
that struggle Christ spoke about
and participated in?
A struggle in which you
together with the others
are helping humanity
and this world
to grow
    by your work,
    by your decisions,
    by your teaching,
    by your honesty,
    by your patience,
    by your respect,
    by your attention
    to those areas
    of human life
    where God's creative plan
    is most frustrated:
      the poor,
      the oppressed,
      the humble,
      and the modest ones.
You are going to be a teacher;
are you going to teach
as he taught?

You are going to be a doctor;
are you going to heal
as he healed?
You are going to be a lawyer;
are you going to judge
as he judged?
You are going to be an engineer;
are you going to build
as he built?
You are going to be an administrator;
are you going to administer
as he administered?
You are going to be a scientist;
are you going to treat nature
as he did
to the benefit of the whole of humankind?
    If you do,
    you will think not only
    of yourself;
    you will renounce that exclusivity,
    you will join him,
    shouldering his cross
    to bring better life
    to all,
    losing that old life
    we know but too well.

   *Tarmack: a verb used by students who walk the tarmacked (paved) streets of Nairobi looking for a job.

33.

CALLED TO FREEDOM

(Luke 9:51–62)

The readings today
are about freedom
and what to do with it.
They are about liberty and liberation,
about freedom and the freedom fight.
They start with that strange story
from the Old Testament:

A boy Elisha
is ploughing
in the field
with his oxen.
A prophet comes along,
a major one,
with a call and a mission.
The prophet calls the young man,
"Come and follow me."
The boy stops his plough,
looks around
to see who is speaking,
and answers:

"Okay, I am coming,
but let me first go and kiss
my father and my mother."
The prophet turns away
and says:
"If that is a condition,
forget about my call;
in that case you are not free
to follow God's call;
in that case you are not free
to be blown by the Spirit."
And the boy did not go
to kiss his father and his mother;
he killed his oxen
on the spot;
he broke his plough;
he barbecued the oxen
on the fire made with the wood
of the plough;
they ate
and they went.
In the Gospel
there are three similar stories
about Jesus,
Jesus the maximum prophet
with his call and mission.
A man came up to him
and said:
"I will follow you,
WHEREVER you go."
And Jesus said:
"I am not going anywhere,
I have no hole like a fox,
I have no nest like a bird,
I have no stone to lay my head on,
I have no fixed abode,
I have no home in this world
and no destination;

CALLED TO FREEDOM 187

I am free to be blown anywhere,
even there where I would not want
to go."
    It seems that the man
    left;
    he did not find
    what he was looking for:
    security, an investment possibility,
    a shamba, a home,
    a protected shelter:
    he was NOT free.
And a second man came along;
this time Jesus took the initiative,
and he said:
"Follow me."
And the man said:
    "Yes, I am coming,
    but let me first bury my father;
    let me be with him till he dies."
And Jesus answered:
"So, you are not free
to leave your father and your mother,
your past and your tradition,
when the kingdom calls;
forget about it."
And a third one came along,
and again Jesus took the initiative
and he said:
"Follow me."
And the man answered:
"Yes, I am coming,
but let me first go back
and greet my folks at home."
    And Jesus said:
    "So, you are not free;
    you say yes,
    but you say yes
    under a condition;

  forget about it;
  it is the Spirit
  and nothing else."
The freedom
he preaches
is absolute and total,
free from the past:
  no burying of the dead;
free from the present:
  no greeting of your folks;
free from the future:
  no fixed place to go.
But is our freedom total,
is our human freedom absolute?
  There was a man who said so,
  and he climbed
  the Kenyatta Conference Centre,
  and he opened a window
  on the seventeenth floor,
  and he shouted,
  "I am free,"
  and he jumped out the window
  to end up
  in front of the building
  like a squashed tomato.
"I am free," said another,
and he went to bars and clubs,
to girls and the wives of his colleagues,
and one day
he came home,
to find no home any more,
because his wife and his children
had gone,
and a home without a wife and children
is no home;
it is a house,
a pile of wood and stones
and a fence.

"I am free," said another,
"I am free to celebrate my freedom,"
and he went to a bar
and he drank all he had,
his money and his cattle,
his *shamba* and his car,
and one evening he staggered home,
he fell in a ditch,
and that night it rained very
heavily,
and he drowned in the gutter
of that street.
"I am free,"
said the man with the machine gun,
and he started to shoot,
and to shoot and to shoot,
and he found himself in the end
alone and lonely,
hiding and at a loss.
"I am free,"
said the student,
and he never opened a book,
and he never went to a lecture,
and he never got a mark either,
in the end of the year
he failed in his
freedom.
We are called to freedom,
but Saint Paul
in his letter of today
to the Galatians and to all Kenyans,
warns us:
"My brothers,"
he wrote,
"you were called to freedom,
but not to self-indulgence;
there is a law,
there is a plan,

there is a line,
there is a limit,
there is a set task:
'serve one another
in works of love.' "
        Everywhere that God's Spirit
        is at work in the Bible,
        there is freedom and liberty,
        freedom to follow,
        freedom to forgive and to forget,
        freedom to build and to order,
        freedom to serve and to love.
My brothers and sisters,
my brothers and sisters,
this is what Saint Paul wrote to you,
Galatians and Kenyans:
        "You were called
        as you know
        to freedom,
        but be careful,
        or this freedom
        will provide an opening
        for self-indulgence,
        and then you will be caught again,
        snapping at each other,
        tearing each other to pieces,
        you had better watch,
        Galatians and Kenyans,
        or you will destroy
        the whole community."
    Peace, not pieces.

34.

THE TWELVE COULD NOT DO IT

(Luke 10:1–20)

Again and again
we hear ourselves
and others say,
when facing the troubles in this world:
"But why does the church not speak out?"
"Where are our leaders?"
Some time ago
a book was launched
over here in Nairobi,
a book by one of the most famous
authors in East Africa,
Ngugi wa Thiongo,
Petals of Blood,
And he too
in very vivid and colorful detail
describes his awareness of that question:
"Why is it that the church leaders
seem to remain so irrelevant
in the struggle of humankind
against the ills of this world?"

When people speak like this,
lay people and priests,
they almost always point fingers
at others.
No finger ever points
at itself.
We point our fingers
at cardinals, bishops,
the pope, or priests.
We are pointing fingers
at the successors
of those twelve disciples
around Jesus Christ.
According to Luke
those twelve disciples
were sent out one day
into the world
by Jesus Christ
to proclaim the kingdom of God,
to cure diseases,
to heal,
to restore,
and to cast out devils.
Before they went,
he called them together
and he instructed them.
He told them
not to take a stick,
not to carry any luggage,
no bread,
no spare shirt,
and no money.
And they went,
and they came back,
and they reported
that they had healed
and restored
and forgiven,

but they complained
that they had NOT been able
to cast out the devils.
    In Luke we find
    another story as well
    about such a mission.
    That story is not about the twelve.
    It is about the seventy-two others.
    Those seventy-two were not the apostles.
    We know the names of the twelve;
    their church-leadership assured them
    an official canonization.
    We don't know the names of those seventy-two;
    they were not part
    of the apostolic or priestly college.
They too were sent out
without a purse,
without a bag,
and barefoot
to announce the kingdom,
to heal the sick,
to restore and to forgive
and to cast out devils.
    It is as if Luke already
    foresaw
    two different functions
    in the church:
    the function of the twelve
    and the function of the seventy-two;
    the function of the leaders
    and the function of the people.
    Luke described not only
    the mission of those twelve,
    the popes, the bishops, and the priests,
    but also the mission
    of the other church members,
    the seventy-two,
    the laymen and the laywomen.

And that "lay" means:
those who form the *laos,*
the people,
the stuff humankind is made of.
When the twelve came back
from their mission,
they complained
that they had not been able
to cast out
the devils.
When the seventy-two came back,
they were rejoicing:
"Lord,"
they said in their report,
"Lord,
even the devils submit to us
when we use your name!"
I would like to suggest
that the difference
in those two reports from Luke
reveals a truth
that remains valid today,
a truth that answers
also
the question
we started this sermon with:
"Should the church leaders not
do more?"
The chasing out of the devils
that tear humankind apart
is a work
that cannot be done
by the church leaders;
even if they spoke out
as they should.
That work cannot be done
by those twelve,
but by the seventy-two,

who together with those twelve
form eighty-four,
that is, seven times twelve,
and that is in the Bible
completion
and perfection.
You, definitely, belong
to the seventy-two.
And that means that you
should be on your
MISSION.
Are you healing?
Are you restoring?
Are you forgiving?
Are you casting out?
      Jesus said:
      "The harvest is rich."
      So many people
      would like to get rid
      of the devils
      in their lives
      and in this world.
Think about the youth
in this nation,
literally millions and millions,
in all kinds of age groups,
asking,
asking,
asking,
What should we do?
What can we do?
Who should we become?
Who can we become?
      "The harvest is rich,
      but the laborers are few."
      There are schools
      in which more than 50 percent
      of the Standard 7 girls are pregnant,

not because they are bad,
not because they are "loose,"
but because they were at a loss.
They did not know what to do
and there was nobody to tell them.
Give a talk to youth
and you will hear
how they bombard you
with their questions.
Who is going to tell them?
Who is going to help them?
Who is going to redeem them?
Who is going to save them?
The bishops,
the cardinals,
the priests,
me?
NO,
not the
twelve,
but the
seventy-two,
you.

35.

WHO IS MY NEIGHBOR?

(Luke 10:25–37)

The story of today
is called the story
of the good Samaritan.
There are four persons
in the story:
     a priest,
     a Levite,
     a Samaritan,
     and one victim,
     the man who was robbed.
With whom of the four
should we identify?
Who should be our example
and model?
The question does not seem
to be difficult.
The answer is easy:
     we should, of course,
     not follow the example
     of the priest.

> When he saw the half-dead man,
> he crossed the street
> to the other side,
> and he made a wide circle
> around the beaten-up man,
> not because he did not want to help,
> but because he thought
> that he was NOT ALLOWED
> to help.

Do not forget
that the robbed man
seemed to be dead.
And did not Scripture say:
"Anyone who touches a corpse
shall be unclean for seven days"?
The priest remembered his regulations
from the Book of Numbers,
and he walked on.

> We should, of course,
> not identify
> with the Levite either.
> He too crossed the street
> and passed on the other side,
> not because he was without mercy,
> but he, also, thought
> that he was NOT ALLOWED
> to help.

Did not the Book of Leviticus say:
"Speak to the Levites and say to them:
none of them is going to make himself
unclean
by going near the corpse
of even one of his family,
unless it be of his closest relatives,
father,
mother,
son,
daughter,

brother,
or his virgin sister."
He remembered this rule
from his seminary years,
and he too crossed the road
as prescribed,
and he walked on.
    And then the Samaritan
    comes along.
    He was moved by compassion.
    He came down from his horse
    or from his donkey,
    he bandaged the wounds,
    he put the man on his animal,
    he brought him to the inn.
    With some difficulty
    he got him a room,
    because the innkeeper insisted:
    "This is not a hospital."
    He paid in cash,
    and he promised to come back
    to settle the eventual difference.
And Jesus
finishes the story
and tells the *lawyer*
who had asked him the question:
"Go and do the same,"
implying:
"Overlook the law
in such a case."
It seems obvious
that we should be
like the ethical hero
of this story,
and that we
enthusiastically
should join the "do-gooders,"
the merciful ones,

the Samaritans,
and all those other people
who spend their lives
caring for others,
the sick,
the handicapped people,
and the orphaned school-leavers.
It seems that we have to join
those
whose photos
we see regularly in the papers
handing,
with broad smiles,
large checks
to children's and other homes.
It seems that we should join
those people of whom we hear
over the radio news
that they gave
30,000, 3,000, 1,000, or 600
Kenyan shillings
for a new school,
a new hospital,
a new church,
a social hall, or something like that.
>   It is as if we are invited
>   to form together
>   one enormous kind
>   of Red Cross,
>   so keen on helping
>   that we start,
>   so to speak,
>   collecting blankets
>   and making coffee
>   an hour
>   before
>   the next disaster strikes.

And yet I wonder
whether that is the whole story,
because Jesus
really asks another question.
He asks:
"Which of those three
proved himself to be
a neighbor
TO THE MAN WHO WAS ROBBED."
>He does not take the point of view
>of the Samaritan;
>he takes the point of view,
>as it is usual with him,
>of the victim,
>of the beaten-up man.
When Jesus asks the question:
"Who is my neighbor?"
he is not asking:
>"Whom am I going to help,
>where are the poor,
>where are the sick,
>where are the lonely,
>where are the prisoners,
>where are the victims,
>where are the miserable ones?"
He is asking
another question.
He is asking:
>"Who is my neighbor,
>who is going to help
>ME?"
>It is I who need help,
>it is I alongside the road,
>it is I waiting for mercy,
>it is I waiting for oil,
>it is I waiting for wine,
>it is I waiting for transport,

it is I waiting for a bed,
it is I waiting for the continuation
of my life,
it is I waiting for meaning,
a meaning that can help me
to stand up and to continue.
And in that case,
starting from that point of view,
the point of view of Jesus,
who is always
with those who suffer
and are oppressed,
the issue is:

Who are *my* neighbors,
who are *your* neighbors?
Who are helping you
to give meaning and sense
to your life:
your husband,
your wife,
your children,
the people you serve,
the people you live for,
those on whom you depend!

The man alongside the road
needed the Samaritan
to save his life,
but the Samaritan
needed the man alongside the road
to fill his life.

We should conclude today
not only
that others need us.
They do.
But we, too, need them,
we need the others.
Who is my neighbor?

They are those I should help,
they are those who help me.
And let us not forget
that in the last instance
it is easier to give
than
to receive!

36.

MARTHA, MARTHA

(Luke 10:38–42)

Some experts
in the history of Bible interpretation
and Bible translation say
that the text:
    "Martha, Martha,
    you worry and you fret
    about so many things
    and yet few are needed,
    indeed only one"
is one of the two most abused and misused
texts in the New Testament.
The second one is,
according to those same experts,
a passage from Matthew:
    "The poor you will have
    always
    with you."
The "Martha, Martha" text
has been used
over and over again
to warn, to judge,
and to depreciate others.

204

It has been used against those
who are always busy:
against husbands
working day and night
to make ends meet;
against housewives
busy to make out of hardly anything
a decent meal
or a "new" dress;
against nurses,
nursing;
against students,
studying;
against farmers,
farming;
against laborers,
laboring;
against authors,
writing;
against priests,
working;
against watchmen,
watching.
It has been used
and it is used
against all those
taken up
by their social work;
against all those
who cannot afford themselves
very often
the luxury of being alone,
of being alone with God,
or of sitting at the knees of Jesus,
listening to him:
the only thing
that really counts.
    It is a text used
    to condemn.

It is a text
that from the beginning
has been causing difficulties,
even while the Bible was being composed,
and while it was finding its
final form.
It is a text
of which the oldest documents
give six different versions.
It is one of those texts
that have given a headache
to all Bible translators.
Mary was the contemplative sister;
Martha was the active one.
Mary was the type of the
New Testament Christian,
living on the grace of Jesus' word;
Martha was the type of the
Old Testament believer,
working according to the law.
Mary was the example of a Protestant,
safe at the knees of the master;
Martha was the example of the Catholic,
working for her salvation.
Martha was good;
Mary was better.
The "Martha, Martha" text
has been used to discriminate
and to condemn.
That is very strange,
because if you have a good look
at the text,
you will see
that in fact
the text condemns
us condemning each other.
It is not difficult
to understand
what happened that day.

It is something
that in one way or another
must have happened
to all of us.
 You are visiting a friend,
 a very dear friend.
 You come unexpectedly.
 You are welcomed,
 embraced and embracing,
 and then,
 when the greetings are over,
 just at the point
 that the *nzuri**
 is going to give place
 to the real news,
 your hostess,
 your friend,
 disappears into the kitchen,
 leaving you alone,
 and because
 you are with many
 you cannot follow her
 to that kitchen.
 And although you came for her,
 you do not see her any more:
  she is making tea,
  baking a cake,
  opening a tin,
  cleaning fruits,
  putting water on the fire,
  and you go to the kitchen
  or you call from the living room:
  "Hey, come here,
  I came for you,
  sit down with me,
  do not make such a fuss,
  do not make it too complicated,
  we do not need very much,
  one thing will do!"

That is what happened;
Jesus arrived;
he was, of course, not alone;
he had his disciples with him;
they went to his very dear friends
Martha and Mary.
Martha welcomes him
very enthusiastically
to disappear
immediately afterwards
into the kitchen,
but Mary stayed with him,
or maybe,
she also
was running up and down
from the kitchen to the sitting room,
to begin with,
but then once
she did not return to the kitchen
and stayed with him.
And then Martha comes from the kitchen,
indignant,
and she tells Jesus
to reproach her sister,
to *condemn* her,
for just sitting there
listening
and doing nothing.
    Jesus refuses
    to condemn Mary,
    and he says to Martha:
    "You are so busy,
    come and sit down with us,
    do not make things too complicated,
    keep it simple,
    one thing will do,
    I did not come for your food,
    I came for you."

But Martha disappeared again
to her pots and pans
to prepare for a meal
that, a bit later,
they all enjoyed very much:
>   Jesus, his disciples,
>   Martha, and Mary.
>   And Jesus must have said
>   after that meal to Martha:
>   "Martha,
>   that was very good,
>   thank you."
Jesus refused to condemn Mary,
who listened to him,
but Jesus did not offer us any reason
to condemn Martha,
who cooked for him,
either.
>   A person who prays
>   CANNOT use this text
>   to judge and condemn
>   those who work;
>   and those who work
>   CANNOT use this text
>   to judge and condemn
>   those who pray.
Each one of us
has his or her vocation,
each one of us has her or his rhythm
of prayer and work,
his or her call,
her or his personality,
and it is TOGETHER
that we hope to realize
the ONE thing
really asked from us,
the ONE thing needed:
his KINGDOM.

> Let us not judge and condemn
> Martha;
> after all
> it is, according to the text,
> Martha
> who welcomed Jesus.
> Let us not judge and condemn
> Mary;
> after all,
> it is, according to the text,
> her food
> he ate.

Let us try to find out
what OUR task is
when confronted with Jesus,
and let us be faithful to it,
keeping in that way,
our way,
the balance between working and praying
as Martha did
in her way,
and Mary
in hers.

Nzuri: all is well.

37.

THE PRAYER PROBLEM

(Luke 11:1–13)

His disciples asked him:
"Lord, teach us to pray!"
Jesus gave an answer.
But when we look around,
it seems to be rather obvious
that he cannot have answered
that question
definitively
or even satisfactorily,
because almost all of us,
in fact, I think, all of us,
are still with that same question:
How should we pray?
When should we pray?
What should we pray?
  If you meet nuns,
  even the contemplative ones
  locked up in their monasteries
  to pray,
  or the active ones
  running from their schools
  to their hospitals,

driving big Landrovers
or carrying shopping bags
through town,
they all have that same question:
"How should we pray?"
When you speak with priests
and reverends,
the old ones
and the young ones
with their Bibles,
their breviaries,
their rosaries and their missals,
they all have that same question:
"How should we pray?"
    When you speak to housewives,
    husbands, bankers,
    farmers, poets, businessmen,
    or schoolchildren and their teachers,
    the question remains the same:
    "How should we pray?"
The question is so urgent
and the need so great
that clever authors,
publishers, and shopkeepers
discovered
long ago
that there is a lot of money
in that problem,
and they make it
too.
    If you go to the Catholic bookshop
    in Nairobi
    and you give yourself
    the time
    to have a good look
    around,
    you will find
    that they stock

not one
or two
or twelve titles
on that subject,
but dozens
and dozens.
If you count
all the books on prayer
together in that shop
you will come to over
a hundred titles.
It is rather amazing,
however,
that his own disciples,
those Jews,
asked him, Jesus,
how they should pray
because in fact
they knew exactly
how to pray
and what to pray.
It had all been laid down
very carefully
and in great detail
in their law.
They had to pray
in the morning,
in the afternoon,
in the evening,
before work,
before meals,
while washing up,
and so on.
Jesus must have been praying
in another way.
They must have noticed
that he prayed differently
and with a greater ease.

He seems not to have believed
in all those regulations
and exercises.
And people even came to him
to complain.
They said:
"John's disciples are always fasting
and doing prayer exercises,
and the disciples of the Pharisees too,
but your disciples go on
eating and drinking."
Jesus did not stick to their rules,
but he did pray;
there is no doubt about that
in the Gospels.
He prayed before his baptism,
he prayed before he chose his apostles,
he prayed before his transfiguration,
he prayed before he was arrested,
he prayed on the cross.
He prayed during the day
and sometimes
even during the night.
But he prayed in another way,
in a new way;
that is what they had noticed.
They wanted to know his secret.
And that is why they came to ask him:
"How should we pray?"
How should we pray?
If you look
at those books in the bookshop
you will see
that they give
all kinds of pieces of advice.
You should sit down
with crossed legs
in the lotus position.

You should stand on your head
so that your blood
flows into your tired
and bloodless brains.
You should murmur words,
which you repeat
over and over again.
You should use pictures
and beads and flowers.
You should close the curtains
or open them.
You should look
very long
at one point on the wall.
You should meditate for at least
one hour
in the morning.
You should use incense
or candle-light
or soft, religious
background music.
You should dance
and sing,
touch and smell,
and I don't know what.
How should we, however,
pray?
When they asked Jesus,
he did not give them a method.
He did not give them a rule.
He did not indicate any exercise.
He did not say anything
about a posture.
He did not give them
a string of beads
or something like that.
He indicated
an ATTITUDE.

He simply said:
"You should say to God:
Father!"
And in fact
that is NOT what he said.
He really said
that we should call God
ABBA,
and that means:
   baba,
   daddy,
   pappa,
   papa,
   pa,
   dad,
   paps.
And if you have that
ATTITUDE,
if you consider
God
really as your father,
you will pray
always,
without any of those techniques.
   Say: Father;
   live: Father;
   practice: Father;
   insist: Father,
   and you will pray
   always
   and everywhere.
Saint Paul,
first a very law-abiding Jew
and later a very zealous Christian,
wrote to the Romans
in a kind of self-confession:
   "We do not even know
   how to pray."

But he added:
"The Spirit in us,
in our inner room,
is doing it for us,
saying:
ABBA,
Father,
Dad!"
Prayer should be normal
and effortless with us.
We should pray always
and everywhere,
even while eating and drinking,
and we will
ALWAYS BE HEARD.
Forget about all those techniques,
whether they are
       African,
       European,
       Asian,
       or American.
Say:
ABBA,
FATHER.
How could a father cheat his children
or not listen to them?
And even if a human father
might do a thing like that,
he,
that Father,
will never abandon us.
And using that word for him,
we will not abandon each other
either,
never,
being brothers and sisters.

38.

YOUR MONEY
OR YOUR LIFE

(Luke 12:13–21)

A man ran up to Jesus.
He was a tortured man.
He was a frustrated man.
He was a wronged man.
He was a diminished man.
His brother
refused to give him
his share
in their inheritance.
    He had only one idea left in his head:
    how do I get that money,
    how do I get my share.
    His mornings
    were pestered
    by that idea;
    his afternoons
    were pestered
    by that idea;

218

and even during the night,
during the whole night,
he was so pestered
by that one and only idea
that he remained turning
over and over,
from his right side to his left side
and from his left side to his right side,
so that he could not sleep.
He was so full
of that question
and that problem
that he went all the way
up to Jesus
with only that idea in his head.
He could not speak about anything else.
So even before saying:
"*Jambo*," "*Habari yako*,"
and "*Nzuri na salama tu*,"*
he asked Jesus:
"Tell my brother
to give me my part
of our inheritance. . . . "
And Jesus refused
to speak that word,
and he explained
why he refused to do so.
He told that man:
"Be on your guard
against avarice.
It does not help a person
in life.
It makes further life
impossible.
It cuts out
further possibilities.
It blocks everything!"

Is it not true
that you,
yourself,
have been saying the same thing
very often
to yourself?
Did you never say
that if you did not have that car
or your status
or your house
or your *shamba*,
you would be freer,
you would be able
to give another shape to your life?
You would be able
to be more liberal
and more faithful
to the people you love
and to the people
who really fill your life?

It is your car
that blocks you.
It is your house
that kills you.
It is your status
that strangles you.
Things took over
in your life.

And then he told them that
other story:
about a man
who did get his part.
He was already rich
when he was blessed
with an absolute bumper harvest,
fantastic;
the coffee had never been so good.
And he said to himself;

"Let me store it up
for myself;
let me build a larger barn,
a bigger warehouse,
an enormous safe,
a strongroom,
for all the things I have
and let me then take
things easy;
let me eat,
and drink,
and sleep,
having a good time,
I,
by myself,
alone.
        And that is what he did.
        He did not look in his *life*
        for any further possibilities
        anymore,
        because of the *things*
        he had,
        because of his part of the inheritance.
He might have done so much.
He could have organized
a very great feast.
He could have adopted
hungry children
and filled his life with joy.
He could have done
all kinds of things.
He did not.
He could not.
He bound himself.
His goods bound him
with very strong strings.
He did not make anything
out of it.

He could not give
any real sense to his life,
even not to the last task
any one has in this life,
to give sense to his death.
To him
death could mean only
absolute and utter disaster.
        Did you ever hear
        that African story
        on how death and sickness
        came into this world?
        In the beginning nobody
        ever died.
        God gave people life
        for some time
        in this world;
        and then,
        after that some time,
        God would call them over
        to his kingdom
        for a fuller life.
        He used to send a messenger,
        a beautiful looking young man
        with the invitation.
        That young man was so beautiful
        because of the beautiful invitation
        he came to bring.
Everybody was
always
very happy to see him,
always
very happy to switch over
from this life to the next.
        Until that young man,
        one day,
        was sent to invite a man,
        a very rich one,

who had just had
a bumper harvest.
He had just pulled down
his old barn
and built a new one,
a huge one.
He had put his harvest
in that barn
and the very night
that all that was ready
the messenger came
with his invitation from God.
But the rich man said
that he was not going to go,
because he still had too much
to eat and to drink
in this life.
And he did not go.
When the messenger went back to God,
God asked him:
"Where is the man I invited?"
He answered:
"He did not come;
he had too much
to be able to come."
            And God became very upset,
            and it is there and then
            that God decided
            to send sickness and old age
            to people
            before his messenger would come.
            He wanted to soften us up,
            to make us loosen slowly
            with dying eyes,
            with dying ears,
            with dying teeth
            the strings attaching us
            to this earth and to this life.

There came a man to Jesus
and he said:
"Tell my brother
to give me my share
of my inheritance,"
and Jesus refused
to say that word.
He did not want to cooperate
in that man's losing his possibilities
and in binding him in such a way
that neither life
nor death
would make any sense to him
in the end.

Jambo: hello; *habari yako:* what's new?; *nzuri na salama tu:* only goodness and
blessing. These are the usual greetings before a conversation starts.

39.

INVEST IN LIFE

(Luke 12:32–48)

The Gospel reading of today
starts by saying:
"There is no need to be afraid."
When you read a bit further,
Jesus explains
what we should not be afraid of.
We should not be afraid of the moment
that the Master
comes to call us from this life;
we should not be afraid of
death.
    That is exactly
    what life insurance brokers say
    when they visit you:
    You should not be afraid of death,
    because if you pay,
    everything will go on
    in your family as before,
    they say,
    if you pay.

Formerly,
in the good old days,
people did not seem to be afraid
of death in the way we are
now.
Specialists say
that in the old African society
people could not even believe
that they would ever die
and be done away with.
In that society
nobody ever spoke about
"MY" life;
everybody spoke about
"OUR" life.
People saw their lives
in connection with the living
and the dead,
connected with those
they had received their lives from,
and connected with those
they had given life to.
  In those days
  life was our life,
  the life of the family,
  the life of the clan,
  the life of the group.
  And because people did not consider
  "HIS" or "HER" life as
  "MINE" only,
  they simply could not die.
It is only when people
get disconnected from their group
and become individualized
and individualistic
that fear of death enters,
because then,
of course,

one will lose
his or *her* life
at the moment of death:
> in that case
> there is nothing to fall back on,
> there is nothing to fall forward on,
> there is nobody to be connected with;
> one is lost.

In the Gospel of today,
Jesus reasons traditionally
when he says:
"There is no need to be afraid,
because the father
is going to give you
the kingdom and life."
> But he also adds
> that very same condition
> of that connection with others:
> "Sell your possessions
> and give alms;
> get yourself a purse
> that does not wear out,
> an investment that does not
> fail you,
> a real life insurance."

He invites us
to invest in life,
because that is what the person does
who gives alms to another.
But that giving of alms
is not the only way
to invest in human life:
> a father educating his children
> is investing in life;
> a mother feeding her offspring
> is investing in life;
> a teacher who teaches well
> is investing in life;

a civil servant who really serves
is investing in life;
and even a president
who presides well
is investing in that very same
human life.
   It is all
   life investment,
   life insurance;
   and if you invest like that:
   do not be afraid,
   you will live;
   even though you die,
   you belong to life.
That investing,
however, should be
well done.
Paul remarks
that it is not sufficient
to give away all one has.
Alms alone do not help;
the alms should be given
with love;
education alone
does not help,
you should educate
with love;
serving alone does not help,
you should serve
with love;
and to love means
to want *the other* well,
to want *the other* to grow;
love is *other-centered*.
      Even a horse knows that.
      If you stroke a horse
      because you admire it,
      the horse will stand in front of you,
      it will not turn away.

But if,
while stroking it,
you become aware of a pleasant feeling
and an enjoyable sensation in your hand,
and you continue stroking it
because of that feeling,
it will walk away,
immediately.
It noticed the change:
you were no longer admiring the horse;
you were thinking of yourself
only.
Do not be afraid;
build yourself a treasure,
in the only way
you can build a lasting treasure
here on earth:
INVEST IN HUMAN LIFE,
and you are safe
because
that human life is the stuff
the KINGDOM OF GOD
is made of,
here
and in the world to come.

40.

FIRE, SWORD, AND BAPTISM

(Luke 12:49–53)

"I have come to bring a fire
to the earth,
and how I wish
it were blazing already!"
    Some of his disciples thought
    that he brought that fire
    to burn the whole world
    with divine dynamite
    or heavenly napalm bombs.
    They asked him,
    that Prince of Peace,
    "Let that village
    that is unwilling to receive you
    be burnt;
    don't be soft,
    let the heavens spit their fire!"
    But he had answered:
    "You have no idea
    of what Spirit you are."

"Do you suppose that I am here
to bring peace on earth?
No, I tell you,
but rather division,"
or as Matthew wrote:
"but rather a sword."
    And up went the swords
    of his disciples
    in what they called their holy wars,
    against the heretics, the Muslims,
    the Protestants, the Catholics,
    the socialists, the communists,
    persecution, inquisition,
    torturing and bloodshed
    all over,
    and in all this
    they appealed to him,
    that giver of life.
    Didn't he say:
    I came to bring a sword?
    Yes,
    but the sword
    he brought:
    was it the one he was
    brandishing,
    or was it the sword
    used against him?
"There is a baptism
I must still receive,
and how great is my distress
till it is over."
    That baptism was his death
    on the cross,
    when those swords of
        the Jews,
        the Romans,
        the Sadducees,
        the Pharisees,

the elders,
the scribes,
the police,
and the people
turned against HIM,
and the enemies
Herod and Pilate
even became friends
to kill him,
because of that fire
that is going to change
the face of this earth,
in him.

41.

THE GATE IS NARROW

(Luke 13:22–30)

Through towns and villages
Jesus went teaching,
making his way
to Jerusalem,
where he was going to be
murdered.
He must have known that.
In a sense it was even the reason
he went.
He was going in
through that narrow door,
death,
over the narrow path leading
to it,
and while he had
this set of ideas
with him,
> there comes that man
> who asks:
> "Sir, will only a few be
> saved?"

233

Jesus did not answer
that question directly.
He never does,
He hardly ever could;
his frame of reference
was too different from that
of his questioners.
He said only:
    "The gate is open;
    it is narrow,
    but it is open;
    everyone
    should be able to pass;
    nobody
    should be left behind."
He said that,
although he had also said
before
and somewhere else
    that it would be easier
    for a camel
    to go through the eye of a needle
    than for some
    to go through that narrow gate.
According to some exegetes,
one of the gates leading into Jerusalem
was so narrow
that a big,
richly loaded camel,
could not pass that gate,
and that gate was nicknamed
the "needle's eye,"
just as we now call
some roads
"bottlenecks."
    The gate is narrow,
    but it is open.

The man wanted to ask,
"How many will you let through,
how many will your kingdom-of-heaven
immigration officers stop?
Who will get a visa,
who will get a residence permit,
who will get a passport,
who will get an identity card,
who will get an alien's registration?"
> His answer was:
> The gate is open,
> free entry,
> no restrictions,
> no bribes,
> no taxes,
> no stamps,
> no complimentaries,
> no watchmen,
> no guards,
> nothing,
> but once more:
> the gate is narrow."
What did he mean?
It was the
richly loaded camel
that could not pass.
Did you never hear that story
about the man
who was warned:
"The police are looking for you,
the CIA, the CID.*
Disappear,
there is still time,
the road is open,
be quick."
But he postponed
and postponed,

because he wanted to arrange
all kinds of things before:
to hide his car,
to bury his gold,
to get his money;
and suddenly
it was too late:
he disappeared.
    During the Second World War
    Jewish families would be warned:
    "Get out,
    disappear,
    you cannot take much,
    the luggage margin is very narrow,
    one piece only,
    be ready tomorrow."
    They were not ready
    that morrow;
    they had not been able to make up
    their minds
    on what to take
    and what to leave,
    and they were taken,
    and they PERISHED.
How many will be saved?
The door is open,
but it is narrow;
the path leading to it
is narrow too;
only PERSONS can pass,
but only PERSONS do matter.
    So let us not make
    all kinds of things our worry
    and burden;
    let us live a human life
    to the full;
    invest all you have in that human life
    in yours and that of others.

Live simple
and sober
and generous;
do not care about what the others
say;
live just and chaste,
simple and uncomplicated.
But LIVE
It is the only thing you have:
your life.
Live,
caring for the only thing
that will pass with you
through that narrow door,
you and those others
you are living with.
        That is what he did,
        on his way to Jerusalem,
        walking the narrow road,
        to that narrow gate
        of his cross
        and the life and glory
        to follow.
        Amen.

*CIA: Central Intelligence Agency; CID: Criminal Investigation Department.

42.

GROWING DYNAMISM

(Luke 14:1, 7–14)

The party was almost on.
Everybody had picked a place.
The host came in.
He had to rearrange the order:
    some had to go up,
    some had to go down,
    honor
    and shame.
    An advice is given.
    At first sight a simple lesson
    in human wisdom:
    if you want to be honored,
    pick the lowest place,
    and you will be honored.
    The advice is on how
    to be honored
    better.
    And that recommendation
    seems to fall out of tune
    with the whole rest of the Gospel.
    How could he have said
    a thing like that?

But the lesson
digs very deep,
much deeper than that.
A movement is recommended,
the movement of God.
All through the Gospels:
he elevates the lowly.
    Mary shouted this out
    in her Magnificat,
    and he said himself
    that he had come
    because of the sinners;
    without them,
    he would not have come.
And God
created
the whole of the universe
out of nothing.
    We should follow that movement
    coming from God;
    it is the real thing,
    it is the way things happen.
    Is it not true that this society
    should change:
        because of the poor,
        because of the children,
        because of the women,
        because of the oppressed,
        because of the lowly,
        because of the landless,
        because of the unemployed,
        because of the slum-dwellers,
        because of the squatters?
And it is in that way
that we might say:
Blessed are the poor;
blessed are we,
because of the poor—
not because poverty is good;

poverty is bad.
And that is the reason
that we will have to move
and to change,
enabling them to move up.
Without them
we would not be under the obligation
to do anything at all,
and the dynamism in the world
would be
nil.

43.

HIS REVOLUTION

(Luke 14:25–33)

The Gospel of today
sounds very harsh
at first hearing:
 to hate your father,
 to hate your mother,
 your wife,
 your children,
 your brothers,
 your sisters,
 and even your own life
 and all your possessions
 in order to follow him;
 it seems too much.
But we must consider
in what kind of context
Jesus was saying all this.
 He was on his way to Jerusalem.
 He was on his way to the cross;
 he was going to be murdered,
 and he knew that very well.

241

And there they were,
the hundreds,
the thousands,
following him on his way
to that cross.
He knew
where this road was leading him,
but they did not know
at all.
And that is why,
once,
and this is the once
the Gospel speaks about,
he turned around
and stopped them.
And he asked them:
"Do you really know
what you are doing?"
In fact
they were following him
for completely different reasons:
    they wanted a change:
    there were the hungry
    who wanted to be fed;
    there were the sick
    who wanted to be healed;
    there were the poor
    who wanted to become rich;
    there were the dead,
    carried by their living relatives,
    who,
    according to those relatives,
    wanted to be revived.
They followed him
enthusiastically,
full of hope
and very interested
in the good things of this life.

He turned around,
he stopped them,
and he said:
"Are you sure
that you are really willing
to walk my way?
Do you know
where I am going?
Did you count the costs,
and are you willing to pay them?"
There was a misunderstanding
between him and his followers.
They were following him
the old way;
they had not changed their options
in life.
They wanted to profit from him,
to get more things,
to get a better position
in the old order,
to get rich
and to get healthy,
to get security in this world
that this world had never been able to offer.
        And he,
        he wanted them to live another life,
        with another option,
        from within another vision.
He wanted a change;
they too wanted a change,
but they wanted another one
than the one he was thinking of.
They were thinking of themselves ONLY,
they were thinking of their families ONLY,
they were thinking of their lives ONLY,
they were thinking of their possessions ONLY.
        And he was thinking of
        the kingdom of God,

the kingdom of people,
the kingdom of the whole of humankind;
he was thinking of humankind
as God's family
on its way
to a final outcome.
He was thinking of a totally different
change.
Nowadays, too,
very many people are thinking
about a change,
a very radical one.
And people have not only been thinking about this.
Profiting from this very deep desire,
leaders have been organizing
sometimes very bloody
and sometimes rather unbloody
revolutions.
Almost the half of humankind
is living in a post-revolutionary
age.
But what did those revolutions
really change?
The names of the leaders changed,
yes;
the names of the leading groups changed,
yes;
the portraits of the presidents
in the public buildings and bars changed,
yes;
but did the human condition change?
Did our option change?
Did we become less selfish?
There was a country far from here,
with a terrible dictator.
He was really sucking the blood
of the poor.
The farmers in that country
got very upset.

They organized themselves,
and they shot that old dictator,
and appointed their own leader
as the new one.
But after some years that new leader
was really a dictator,
and he was really sucking the blood
of the poor,
and the farmers got very upset,
and they organized themselves,
and they shot that old new leader,
and they appointed their own leader
as the new one.
But after some years that new leader
was really a dictator,
and he was really sucking the blood
of the poor,
and the farmers got very upset,
and they . . .
Jesus turned around
to all those
who followed him,
and he asked:
    "Did you change your option
    when you decided to follow me?
    Are you willing to think
    in terms of the kindom of God?
      Are you willing to give up your old ways,
      your own self,
      your brotherization,
      your own life,
      your possessions?"
Can you do that?
Do not try to start to build
a new city,
if you are not willing to do that.
You will shed blood,
very much blood,
and it will be all in vain.

Do not try to start a revolution
or a war
if you are not willing to change
really:
you will fight idly,
nothing will change,
and nothing will be
won.

44.

THEY WERE ANGRY

(Luke 15:1–32)

They were angry with Jesus,
the good ones,
the clean ones,
the law-abiding ones,
the well-washed ones,
the learned ones,
the faithful ones,
the temple-goers.
    They were angry
    because he sat down at his table with
      the bad ones,
      the dirty ones,
      the disobedient ones,
      the careless ones,
      the stupid ones,
      the faithless ones,
      and with those who were never seen
      in the temple
      or a synagogue.
They made no secret of their thoughts;
they complained bitterly,
and they blamed him.

And then he tells them those three stories,
three very strange stories,
about a man who leaves
ninety-nine obedient sheep alone,
to look for one crazy one;
about the housewife
who does not bother about the nine coins
in her apron pocket,
but turns her whole house over
to look for one lost one;
and about a father,
who organizes a party
for his good-for-nothing son
and who even forgets to inform
his faithful son
about it.
They were very angry!
Why?
Just imagine that Jesus
sent today a heavenly messenger,
Gabriel or Michael or Raphael,
to inform us,
that he would come over here to Nairobi
to visit us at the end of the month.
Don't you think
that in such a case
all churches would prepare,
the choirs would renew their repertoire,
the buildings would be repaired,
everything would be freshly painted,
the paint would be donated,
the large churches
and the small ones,
the old ones and the independent ones,
would wash their stoles,
their vestments, their cassocks and albs,
their banners, their flags, and their streamers,
and everybody would live in expectation.

And then he comes,
he really comes,
but
    he does not go to All Saints Cathedral,
    he does not go to Holy Family Cathedral,
    he does not go to the Deliverance Church;
    he goes to the *changaa* and *busaa* drinkers,*
    he sits down in nightclubs with girls,
    and he invites bribers and thieves and smugglers
    to his table.
What would the reaction be?
What would your reaction be?
Their reactions were clear.
They could not stand it.
They had thought that they were
the sacred ones,
the privileged ones,
the chosen ones,
and the saved ones.
Saint Luke wrote somewhere else
in his Gospel (18:9):
"They were sure of their own goodness,
and they despised anyone else."
They thought that they had fulfilled the law;
    they were the sheep
    that had always been obedient;
    they were the coins
    that had always remained in the purse;
    they were the son
    who had always stayed at home;
    and now they were not even
    invited,
    informed,
    or preferred.
And in the end
they killed him
to prove that they were right
and that he was wrong,

that they were the blessed ones
and that he was the cursed one.
Under the cross they shouted:
"Now save yourself,"
"Let us see whether God is
going to save him."
> They killed him
> because he had forgiven
> the others;
> they killed him
> because he had invited
> the others
> to his table.
They could not stand
that God was greater
than their hearts;
they could not stand
that God is good
for the wicked.
They thought that they had done
everything,
because they had reduced
God's lifestyle
to their own law.
> They did this so many times,
> they did that so many times,
> they went to the synagogue
> every sabbath,
> they prayed all the prescribed
> prayers,
> they never ate pork,
> everything was kosher,
> they were all right . . .
But did you
ever
realize the nature of
Christ's prescriptions?

They cannot be fulfilled
completely,
never:
> forgive seven times seventy times;
> if anyone slaps you on your right cheek
> turn to him
> your left cheek.
> They cannot be fulfilled.
> He did not even fulfill them
> himself.
> When they slapped him,
> he did not turn his cheek;
> he protested:
> "Why do you beat me?"

His measure
will never be reached
by any one of us.
We will always depend on him,
> who is looking for the stray sheep,
> for the lost coin,
> for the lost son,
> for us,
> who are all
> invited to that table
> of his.

Changaa and *busaa*: illegally brewed drinks.

45.

SMALL THINGS

(Luke 16:1–13)

The Gospel reports on Jesus
are,
from one point of view,
as one-sided
as all other books
and reports
and films:
  they speak only
  or speak almost exclusively
  about "high" things,
  about "important phases,"
  and about "decisive decisions"
  in the life of Jesus.
  The "normal" things,
  the ordinary things,
  are overlooked.
They are about miracles,
and hardly ever about everyday life.
They are about significant temptations,
so significant that the devil himself
is seen,

and not about the type of temptations
that pester us
all through the day.
They are about paramount decisions,
and not about the common daily ones.
Of course,
we know that he had been living
in Nazareth
for about thirty years.
But the Gospels hardly speak
about them.

     As a small boy,
     while reading the books about my heroes,
     I was already asking myself
     about the normal and common things
     in the lives of those cowboys and red Indians.
     They jumped from adventure to adventure,
     they never needed sleep,
     they never took a cup of coffee,
     only bottles full of whiskey;
     they never needed to go to a toilet,
     they never washed their faces
     or brushed their teeth;
     they never seemed to have children;
     they always lived at peak hours,
     in peak times,
     on peak days.
And almost all reports
we write or hear or see
about other people
do the same.
We hear about queens and kings,
about presidents and generals,
only when they decide to imprison,
to liberate, to kill, or to murder.
And if we,
ourselves,
want to get some publicity,

we, too, must do something very big,
something extra-ordinarily stupid,
or something unbelievably clever.

> And nobody counts
> the glasses of water,
> the cups of coffee,
> the "good" mornings,
> the baby diapers changed,
> the school hours,
> the friendly (and unfriendly) words,
> the hours in the kitchen,
> the bread baked,
> the *matoke* steamed,*
> the rice sifted,
> the coins changing hands,
> the papers turned in offices,
> the hands laid on heads,
> the sick visited,
> the efforts and the failures,
> the attempts and the successes
> of our everyday lives.

And that is why very many people,
and not only the young ones,
reading those books,
seeing those films,
paging through those pages
telling their stories,
feel themselves small and fenced in,
dissatisfied and frustrated,
and they are waiting for the day
that their hour of fame and glory
will come.

> And Jesus says today,
> in the Gospel,
> that that hour will never come,
> and that, if it comes,
> we will not be ready for it
> if we cannot be trusted in those small things,
> because he says:

"The person
who cannot be trusted
in small things,
cannot be trusted
in great things either.
It is only the person
who can be trusted
in small things
who can be trusted
in those great things."
All the martyrs
and the confessors
and the saints
and the heroes
were able to make their
"great decisions"
because they were building on all those
small decisions
in little things.
Somewhere in the Old Testament
people had been complaining
about the slowness with which
the new temple was built.
The prophet Zechariah told them:
"Indeed, we live in the days
of little things,
no doubt about that,
but who would dare despise them?"
The temple will be finished,
one stone on top of the other,
millions of years of human life,
tens of thousands of hours
in everybody's life,
millions of words,
decisions,
small things,
grains of sand,
but the kingdom,
the temple, is being built:

a kingdom that depends
on a glass of water
given or refused:
"Since you have been faithful
in very small things,
I will give you the kingdom.
Amen!"

    Matoke: banana stew.

46.

THE HOUR OF THE POOR

(Luke 16:19–31)

The story of the Gospel of today
is a very simple story.
It is a very well-known story too.
There is that rich man
sitting in the middle of his cool house,
surrounded by musicians and dancers,
smartly dressed
in fine imported clothing,
in purple and silk and linen,
making a real impression
on his extraordinarily high platform shoes.
Jesus said
that he feasted
every day:
kilos of meat,
buckets of champagne,
and at night he slept
in a bed made of pure ivory.
    The poor Lazarus
    is sitting at his door,
    baking in the heat of the sun,

257

without clothing,
a loincloth only,
no shoes,
a dry mouth,
an empty stomach
and a skin infested with
ulcers,
pimples,
wounds,
and sores.
And between the two is that enormous distance,
that wide gap between the rich and the poor,
a gulf as wide and deep
as the Great Rift Valley.*
The poor man cannot even move,
because if he moves,
the dogs of the rich man
start to howl and to growl,
and the rich man never, never moves;
he only sits there,
very stable and very solid,
eating and drinking,
feasting and gaining.

The only ones
that now and then
bridge the gap
are those dogs,
when they come from under the table
of the rich man,
to lick
the ulcers,
the pimples,
the wounds,
and the sores
of Lazarus.
They both die,
they are both buried,

one with
and the other without
pomp and circumstance,
and they both arrive in that mysterious life
after death.
          According to Jesus' story
          everything is changed.
          Only one thing remained unchanged:
          the big gap.
          The rich man is now hungry and thirsty,
          very dry and very hot in an
          overheated hell,
          and Lazarus is sitting
          in the lap of Abraham,
          dressed in silk and gold,
          with plenty of food
          and plenty of drink.
          But the gap remained as wide as before,
          a gulf as wide and deep
          as the Great Rift Valley.
The rich man is unable to bridge that gap,
and the poor man is not able
either.
It is this Gospel story
that according to very many
has been used by preachers and Christians
over and over again
to keep the poor poor,
and the rich rich,
and the gap between them
a gap.
According to them,
this text has been used by a church
that depended on the rich
to defend the so-called law and order,
to defend the so-called prosperity,
status quo, and stability.

The poor were told:
keep your eyes down,
keep your hands folded,
keep your knees bent,
keep your stomachs empty,
keep your mouths dry;
your hour will come,
later,
your hour will come
soon
in heaven,
the hour of the poor.
But the story tells exactly
the opposite,
because when we read further,
it is obvious
that the rich man in that hot hell
began to understand
that he had ended up in hell
because he went wrong
on earth.
He understood that he was in hell
because of his stupid,
egoistic behavior.
He knew that so well
in the long run
that he even wanted to bribe Lazarus
in order to send a heavenly messenger
to his five brothers
who were still on earth,
feasting,
to warn them
and to make them
change their lives,
to ask them
to let others participate
in their work,

their development,
and their prosperity.
    This Gospel story
    cannot be used to tell the rich:
    remain as you are,
    or to tell them that the situation
    should remain as it is.
This is not a Gospel
about stability;
it is a Gospel
that wants to bring in this world
a change-over,
a revolution,
a development,
that is based on the very presence of the poor
among us.
    Brother or sister,
    reading these lines,
    is it not true,
    that it is that presence
    of the poor and the oppressed
    among us
    that should make us move
    and change?
    A move and change that mean
    salvation and redemption
    to them,
    but to us as well.
    The hour of the poor
    is the hour
    of our liberation.

*The Great Rift Valley: a geological fault running from the Dead Sea deep into Africa, dividing Kenya in two.

47.

INCREASE OUR FAITH

(Luke 17:5–10)

The disciples came to Jesus
and they said:
"Lord,
increase our faith!"
I am sure
that very many of us
would like to tell him
that very same thing:
"Lord,
increase our faith!"
  Because we, too, have our doubts:
  about the existence of God,
  about the authenticity of Jesus.
  Was there an apple
  and a talking snake?
  Did the sun stop?
  Were the ten commandments in stone?
  Was the tomb empty?
  Was Mary taken up,
  Was Peter meant to be the head?
  Is sex outside marriage
  a mortal sin?

Do angels have wings?
Am I saved? . . .
and so on.
People will say:
I have so many doubts,
sometimes I give in;
what should I do?
Help me to increase my faith,
please.
>And Jesus gave a very strange answer.
>He did not start to speak
>about any doctrine or dogma.
>He said:
>>"Start moving.
>>If you have faith,
>>do something.
>>Say to that mountain: move,
>>and it will move;
>>say to that old tree
>>that is in your way:
>>walk,
>>and it will uproot itself
>>and walk."
For him faith was not
adhering to a doctrine,
chanting a creed,
but a reality that makes
things happen.
For him a belief
is something
operational.
And he is right!
>A student comes to register;
>he has a look at the registration forms;
>he sees the word "mathematics,"
>or "statistics";
>he looks up and says:
>"Sir, I can't do mathematics,
>you know."

That is his belief,
and, indeed, he will not be able
to do it,
not because he can't,
but because he believes
he can't.
Your friend is in the hospital,
he is very sick;
you talk to him,
you encourage him,
but he says:
"This is the end,
this is the end,
this is the end."
And he turns his head away from you;
he has no belief in his healing,
and he will not heal.
     If you ask that doubtful student,
     "Do you believe in mathematics,"
     he will say:
     "I believe."
     If you ask your sick friend,
     "Do you believe in health,"
     he will say:
     "I believe in health."
     But that type of belief
     does not help them
     at all.
Mathematics is something there
outside of him;
health is something there
outside of him.
     They believe in it
     as in a reality
     that does not touch them,
     that does not help them.
It is in that way
that many Christians
believe

in Jesus,
in the Father,
in the Spirit,
in the saints,
in baptism,
in the resurrection,
in prayer.
All those "things"
remain outside of them,
objectively,
printed in booklets,
hymns, and catechisms.
But ask them:
"What about you,
you,
does it make you move,
does it help you,
does it make you do things?
Did you ever move
a mountain
or a tree
or an obstacle
because you believe?"
And mind you,
Jesus does not say
that GOD will move
that mountain
or that tree
or that obstacle
if YOU believe.
Jesus says that
YOU
with the power of God
will do it.
When Mao Tse-tung
wrote his famous red booklet,
he too spoke about that mountain
in the Gospel reading of today.
And he said:

"People have prayed
for generations and generations
that the mountains would move,
but the mountains have not moved.
People have asked God
for centuries and centuries
for protection against
their flooding rivers,
and nothing happened.
Their faith has not helped."
And he added:
"Now we are going to do it
by ourselves."
And he and the Chinese started,
and the mountains were moved,
and the rivers got their dikes.
Their faith became
operational,
and they forgot that
God had given them the power
to do so.
Do you believe?
Yes, you do.
But do you believe
in Jesus,
his message,
his charity,
his love,
and in his Spirit,
in such a way
that it works
in your life,
in your relationships with others,
in your education,
in the spending of your money,
in your self-respect,
in your studies,
in your planning,
and in your activity?

If it does,
you will be able to remove
mountains,
trees,
and rivers.
If you do,
he will always be with you
and nowhere else,
in you,
a Spirit
you have to fan,
through your belief,
into a burning fire:
in an ever-increasing
faith
that works.

48.

DEEPER THAN THE SKIN

(Luke 17:11–19)

There they were standing
at the prescribed distance from him.
Misery had brought them together,
nine Jews and one Samaritan.
They were not allowed to approach him.
From a distance they shouted:
"Heal us, please, heal us!"
Jesus kept to the rules,
that time,
and he said:
"Go to the priests to show yourselves."
They turned around
and went,
and on their way
they were healed.
    Then one of them,
    number ten,
    came back,
    and he fell before Jesus
    and he thanked him
    at the top of his voice.

That is why
everybody almost always
tells us
that this Gospel episode
teaches us
that we should be thankful.
And definitely:
thankfulness
is a very great virtue.
It shows what a person is worth.
And yet is this story
really about thankfulness?
 They were ten.
 One is called a stranger
 by Jesus,
 a Samaritan.
 When they asked him
 for his help,
 he sent them to the priests in Jerusalem,
 to the Temple skin-disease checking point.
 They went,
 they were healed on their way,
 and it was only then
 that the Samaritan remembered
 that he could not go to those priests.
 He would have been most unwelcome,
 he certainly would have been kicked out,
 and that is why he left the others
 and he returned,
 the only way he really could go.
He came to Jesus to thank him,
but that is not all that happened.
Jesus asked him:
"Where are the others?
The nine others where are they?"
 Of course he knew where they were.
 One had been a shopkeeper
 before his sickness hit him,

and an hour after having obtained his healing
and his health certificate
he was back in his shop,
doing the accounts.
Another one had been a farmer,
and next day he was milking his cows.
Another one had been a lecturer
at the university,
and he too returned directly to his job,
and he was seen in the Senior Common Room
with all his friends.
They all had been touched by Jesus,
their skin,
the surface of their bodies
had been healed,
but for the rest
it had all remained the same.
Now and then,
surrounded by their friends,
in the evening hours,
with a glass of wine in their hands,
they would witness:
"Look at my skin;
once it was one pimple and ulcer and wound.
Jesus touched me,
he healed me,
alleluia,
alleluia,
praise the Lord."
But otherwise
it was as if nothing
had happened.
The Samaritan
came back,
and Jesus said:
"Stand up,
go on your way,
your *faith*
has saved *you*."

Not his skin,
but him;
not the surface,
but his heart;
not his epidermis,
but his mind,
and he followed him,
really.
>   Number ten came back;
>   he did not return
>   to his old life
>   and his old world;
>   he lived a new life
>   with him.
We, too, are all touched by him.
If we had not been touched,
we would not be here.
But how deep did it go?
Are we of the sort of the nine,
or are we like number ten?
>   The nine were tested
>   in their old world
>   according to the old rules
>   in the temple,
>   and they were declared
>   clean and healthy
>   on the surface of their skins.
Number ten
was tested by Jesus,
who said
YOU are healed
and changed.
Number ten never returned
to his old life anymore.

49.

JUSTICE DONE

(Luke 18:1–8)

Jesus told them a story,
a story about a judge.
I am sure that he was using a story
that everybody knew,
because it had happened
one of those days.
And I am also sure
that if he were preaching over here
today
he would have used a Kenyan story
about an unjust magistrate
in this land.

>The judge of the story
>refused to do justice
>to a widow,
>and he had irritated that lady
>up to the point
>that she could not keep
>her hands in her lap any more,
>and she hit out at the judge
>>(because that is what the Greek text
>>literally says)

and she had given him a black eye,
and then he did her justice.
And Jesus says:
"If even an unjust man
does justice
under such a threat
and after so much pestering,
don't you think
that God,
who according to psalm 72,
'rescues the poor
who call to him,'
will do justice?"
And so we should pray for justice,
and I think that we are quite willing
to pray for justice,
because so much injustice today
is done
by others.
That is one of the strange things
about injustice:
it is always done by others,
or it always depends totally
on the socio-economic structure
in which we live.
Justice in this country
is violated
by the multinationals,
and indeed it is violated by them;
justice in this world
is violated by the political systems,
and indeed it is violated by those systems;
justice on this continent is violated
by imperialistic capitalism,
and indeed it is violated
by imperialistic capitalism;
justice in this world is violated
by neocolonial oppression,
and it is true that it is violated
by neocolonial oppression.

And we should pray
that all that will be broken up
and that it may disappear;
we should pray
that justice be done
to the poor, to the needy,
the old and the young,
the widows, and the orphans,
and we will be heard,
we will be heard.
And if we start to be heard,
we will be heard
in the very first place
by ourselves,
because is it really justified
to say
that the injustice
in this world,
on this continent,
in this country,
in this town,
depends
ONLY
on the socio-economic structures
as such?
Does it depend only on
what *others* do?

>Let me tell you a story,
>to make my point clear.
>A story!

A student knocks at my door,
he comes in, he sits down,
and says:
"Father, I cannot find a job."
I say: "No job?"
He says: "No job.
I have been tarmacking* since I left;

all the others had friends,
influential friends,
I have nobody.
This country is unjust,
it does not take merit into account,
it does not offer equal chances,
no justice is done.
Can you please write a letter for me,
because you are very influential,
I think,
so that . . ."

    Does it depend only on the
    socio-economic structures
    that the stoppers in the washbasins
    disappear into the pockets of people
    who want to be sure
    always to have a stopper
    at hand?
Does it depend only on the
socio-economic structures
that showerheads go the same way,
that pages are torn out of library books,
that bulbs, curtains, and furniture are "displaced"?
Is it due only to those structures
that money is wasted,
that food is thrown away,
and that it is often naive
to trust each other?
  Jesus said:
    "Pray for justice
    consistently,
    and it will be given to you
    by your Father
    in heaven
    and even by those
    who are unjust
    now."

If we pray for justice,
we will have no other way out;
we will become just ourselves,
because that is the only way
that prayer
can be heard
by God.

*See footnote to sermon 32.

50.

NOT LIKE HIM

(Luke 18:9–15)

Everybody knows the story of today.
It seems to be a very simple story.
Two men went to the temple;
one was a Pharisee,
the other one a tax-collector.
    The Pharisee said:
        "I am very happy
        that I am not like the rest of humankind.
        I am not greedy,
        I am not unjust,
        I do not commit adultery,
        I fast twice a week,
        and I pay church tax on all I get."
    The tax collector said:
        "I am a sinner;
        I am like the rest of humankind.
        I am greedy,
        I am unjust,
        I do commit adultery,
        I never pay tax,

277

I dodge what I can dodge,
and I even know how to dodge
because I am a tax collector myself."
And the story then concludes
that the first one
in front of the temple
was wrong
and that the second one
in the back of the temple
was right.
Most probably every one of us
is quite willing to agree with that,
and I think that almost all of us
are even willing to add:
"I am very happy that
I am not like that Pharisee,
making in that way the mistake
the Pharisee
made:
thinking ourselves better
than the others
and despising them
for that reason."
But what do you mean when you say
that you are glad not to be like him?
We normally say that he was a hypocrite.
Jesus did not say that.
Jesus did not call him by that name.
He really *was* just.
He really *did* fast twice a week,
though there was no such obligation
in the Jewish law.
He really *paid* temple tax,
not only on grain, oil, and wine,
as prescribed by the law,
but even on the smallest items
like herbs and spices.

And he did pay that tax not only
on the things he sold,
as was foreseen,
but even on the things he bought.
He really *never* went to bed
with another wife than his own.
He was not pretending,
he was telling the truth,
that is what he did.
He went wrong
in something else,
and it is that something else
we should check ourselves on
when reading this text.
The text says:
The Pharisee stood there,
and he prayed *to himself*.
He had gone to the temple,
but he did not pray to God;
he prayed to himself,
he glorified in himself,
he showed himself
why God *should* respect and love him.
It was HE
who was in the center
of his prayer.
He said:
"I thank you God,
that I . . ."
and so on.
It is there that he went wrong.
You cannot tell somebody
to love you,
not even because of all the things you did.
Love does not work like that.
There was a man called Mwaura
and a girl called Wanjiku,

and Mwaura told Wanjiku
that he loved her very much,
but Wanjiku was not so sure.
So he bought shoes for her,
and stockings, food and sugar,
a hair-straightener, vaseline,
and nail polish,
earrings and all kinds of bangles,
and then he told her:
"You should love me;
look at all the things I bought for you."
And she made love with him,
and yet she was not so sure
that she loved him
or even that he loved her
or only himself.
So he bought a flat for her
and a car and a fridge
and a very expensive sofa set,
and again he told her:
"You SHOULD love me;
look at all the things I did for you."
And yet she was not so sure.
All came from him,
but love can neither be proved
nor bought like that.
The more you try to buy love,
the more you try to force others to love you,
the less you will succeed.
Love is something that is given
and neither bought
nor sold.
It is something free
and not a price to be paid.
To force it
is to destroy it.
    And we should love God,
    as we love people,

and we can love God
only as we love people.
That is why Christ said
that the love for God
and the love for people
are the same.
That is where the Pharisee went wrong.
He walked up to the temple,
and he said to himself:
"O God, you should love me,
you should respect me,
look at what I did for you:
I did this
and I did that;
I did not do this
and I did not do that.
Look at me,
a wonderful performer.
Do you love me now?"
    And God kept silent
    because God wanted to love him,
    not because he was paid,
    not because he was forced,
    but because he loved.
God's love started it all.
It started us,
our lives,
our gifts,
our world,
and it is starting from that love
that we can work.
    We should be just
    and pious
    and devout,
like the Pharisee,
not to force God to love us,
but because he is doing so already.
That is what the tax collector understood.

He left the initiative to God;
he said:
    God let it come from you;
    have mercy;
    let it start from you.
    And he went home,
    justified,
    and that means
    that he was going to be
      just
      and pious
      and devout
      like the Pharisee,
      but with
      a difference.

51.

COME DOWN

(Luke 19:1–10)

When Zaccheus heard
that Jesus was going to enter town,
he closed the drawers of his desk
and locked them;
he closed the door of his safe
and locked it;
he closed the door of his office
and locked it;
he closed the door of his house
and locked it;
he closed the gate in front of the house
and locked it;
before he had left his house
Zaccheus had used almost a dozen keys.
He was a money man;
all he thought of was money,
it was about money he dreamt.
    He went into the street;
    he wanted to "see" Jesus,
    but that was all;
    he wanted to "observe" him;

he did not want to be touched by him,
he did not want to be
   pulled,
   pushed,
   admonished,
   or converted by him.
He wanted to "observe" only,
he did not even want to be seen,
he definitely did not want to get involved.
And even before the street started to fill up,
he, therefore, climbed a tree,
and there he sat,
on a branch,
waiting
and thinking about his favorite subject:
MONEY.
So often
every one of us
resembles that Zaccheus
on his branch,
in that tree,
observing only:
   the church should have done this,
   the theologians should have said that,
   the bishops should have written a letter,
   the intellectuals should have started research,
   others,
   others,
   others.
We are sitting in a tree
above reality,
looking down on others
speaking about the *Catholic Society*
and what they should do,
about the *Christian Union*
and what they should do,
about the *Young Christian Students*
and what they should do,

about the *Cardinal*
and what he should do,
not involving ourselves really,
but only observing coolly,
like Zaccheus
WANTED to do.
He did not succeed.
      Then Jesus did enter the street.
      People were milling around him.
      He stopped under the tree,
      he looked up,
      he saw Zaccheus in the tree,
      and he called him:
      "COME DOWN,
      AND HURRY!"
Zaccheus almost fell out of the tree,
and he,
joyfully,
received Jesus.
And he became so enthusiastic
that even before Jesus
had said anything,
he started to respond to him,
spontaneously,
but,
of course,
only in the terms he knew,
in terms of money.
      Zaccheus said:
      "I will give half my capital
      to the poor.
      I will restore everything I stole
      fourfold."
      Money,
      he spoke only in terms of money.
But then Jesus took over,
and Jesus did as if he had not even heard
the word "money" mentioned.

He spoke about the person,
that human being,
his own creation,
Zaccheus.
He gave him a name;
he called him:
SON OF ABRAHAM,
and that name opened
      in Zaccheus,
      that short,
      one-dimensional,
      money-making,
      money-lending,
      money-loving,
      money-smelling
      money-man,
      quite another,
      a new dimension.
      That name "son of Abraham"
      spoke of him in terms
        of eternity,
        of infinity,
        of an eternal promise,
        of divine life,
        of heavens,
        and realities like that.
That same invitation
is today addressed to us:
      COME DOWN,
      come down to join me
      and to open yourself
      to your real dimensions
      and possibilities.
Let us not restrict ourselves
to be observers only;
let us not restrict ourselves
to money and our biological needs only.

Everything around us,
the papers and their advertisements,
the radio and the conversations in the bars,
tries to convince us
that we can be reduced,
to food and drink,
to gold and silver,
to clothing and sex,
to a car and a house,
to beer and Coke,
to soaps, to grants,
and boom.*

    We are larger,
    we are bigger,
    we are absolute,
    we are divine,
    we are sons and daughters of God;
    even heaven is not our limit,
    God himself is our limit.

      And if that is true,
      let us come down
      and respect in ourselves and in each other
      that heavenly country,
      that divine echo.

*boom: the word used by the students of the University of Nairobi to indicate their loan-money.

52.

LAUGHING ABOUT LIFE AFTER DEATH

(Luke 20:27–38)

Today we start the last Sundays
of this liturgical year.
Very soon we will be, again,
preparing for Christmas.
These last Sundays are
very logically
about the end
because the end is,
after all,
the end.
They are about death and resurrection.
In the report from Luke
today,
 a group of people
 called Sadducees
 came to Jesus.
 Sadducees do not believe
 in life after death,
 and they came to ridicule Jesus
 and to laugh at him
 and his after-life ideas.

And I am sure
that the same would happen
to you
if you were to express very clearly
your belief in life after death
on this campus of the University of Nairobi.
  Some will come to laugh
  at you.
  They will ask you:
  "Do you believe in heaven,
  do you believe in the resurrection,
  do you believe in a world after this world?"
  And they will start to ridicule:
   "If after-life exists,
   why did nobody ever
   come back from it?
   If heaven is eternal,
   what are we going to do?
   Sing alleluia
    the first day,
    the second day,
    the first week,
    the second week,
    the first month,
    the second month,
    the first year,
    the second year,
    the first century,
    the second century,
    alleluia,
    always?
   If heaven is a banquet
   or a party,
   who is doing the cooking,
   who is doing the brewing,
   who is doing the serving,
   where do we throw the bones,
   who is going to do the washing up,
   what about the latrine-pits?

If we rise with bodies and souls,
like Jesus and Mary,
on what floor do we stand,
what air do we breath,
where do we get the oxygen?"
And so on.
They will laugh at you;
they will laugh at your ideas,
and very often it is difficult to see
how to answer them.
And next to all that
they always have
that other remark,
one of the best-known remarks about religion
in this world:
the remark that
heaven and hell are used
to make us overlook
the realities of this world;
that heaven and hell are a conspiracy
of the capitalistic world
and its churches
to make us forget
that we are in this world,
that justice should be done over here,
and that all that heaven and hell talk is
a dream,
opium,
a sedative,
a soporific,
religious "changaa"
and pious "bang."
And they will tell you
that Christians too often sing
that very strange hymn:
"I am not of this world."
The Sadducees came to Jesus
to ridicule him
in that very same way.

They wanted to have a good laugh
at his after-life concepts.
They did it very cleverly,
they used a pious tactic,
they started with the Bible,
and they said:
"Master, you know
about that law from Moses
we have in writing
that if a man dies without children,
his brother should marry her
in order to get children
for his dead brother.
Did you get it?"
And Jesus said:
"I got it."
And then they started their story
      about that woman who married a man,
         who died,
         and then his first brother,
         who died,
         and then his second brother,
         who died,
         and then his third brother,
         who died,
         and his fourth,
         and his fifth,
         and his sixth,
         and they all died,
         and then finally,
         she too died,
         of exhaustion,
         I suppose.
And after that story,
they asked him triumphantly:
"What is that woman going to do
in the case of after-life,
after her resurrection
in the life to come?

Live with seven husbands,
she alone,
how is she going to do
a thing like that?"
    The people
    around Jesus
    who had listened to the story
    tried to find a better place,
    not only to hear him,
    but even to see him
    answering that question.
    They were curious,
    they winked at each other;
    how was he going to tackle this one?
He tackled it
in a very profound way.
He did not say
what might happen in the life to come.
He said only
what definitely will not happen over there.
He said:
"It will be over there NOT
like over here;
nobody will be married;
it is a life that transcends
this life!"
And our belief in the resurrection
is exactly that:
    there is more to life
    than our life over here.
    He even explained
    why we will not be married.
    We will not be married
    because nobody dies over there,
    and you marry in this world,
    only to survive in it
    even after your death.

And then, as if to overcome
immediately
that second remark,
about the idea of heaven
being a soporific
in this world,
he added
that the life after this life
is related to this life:
"Only those judged worthy
will rise."
And the others,
he does not say anything
about those others,
but it is implied that they
will not rise
because they lived
unworthily.
    That is all he says,
    and that is all he could say.
    To believe in the resurrection
    is the belief that there is another
    type of life
    awaiting us,
    and if you ask
    for a description,
    that description
    cannot be given.
If they ask:
    "Will we sing,
    is there music,
    a floor,
    ceiling,
    food,
    do we get breakfast,
    do we sleep,
    how many in one room?"

there are no answers possible
to those questions,
and all the answers given
    about heaven or hell
    should be seen
    not as descriptions of reality
    but as examples and metaphors.
Nobody ever came back,
because nobody would be able to say
in this world:
"I AM DEAD."
    But Jesus made it clear:
    live a worthy life
    IN THIS WORLD,
    and you will be living
    forever and ever.

Changaa: a strong drink; *"bang":* marijuana-like intoxicant.

53.

THE END OF THE WORLD

(Luke 21:5–19)

The idea and belief
that the end of the world
and the return of Jesus
are very near
has very often played
havoc
in the lives of many.
    Even this year
    quite some students
    did not qualify for university entry
    because they had been walking around
    with small booklets in their pockets,
    printed in the USA,
    that said
    that the end would come this year
    in the month of February.
    They failed because they stopped
    studying
    to prove
    that they believed.

When we hear such a story,
we very often laugh.
Should we laugh?
They are definitely
in very good company:
>everybody can still read
>in the letters of Paul
>how he believed
>in the beginning of his apostolic career
>that Jesus would return
>during his lifetime.
>And some Bible experts hold
>an even more remarkable theory:
>that Jesus too
>expected the end
>very soon.
>But the date,
>he said,
>he did not know.
It is on the point
of that date
that those Christians
seem to go wrong.
They say that they know,
but it is proved again and again
that they do not know.
They forget,
or they never understood,
that time is a very strange
reality:
>we have the time of
>our clocks and watches,
>the time in which every minute
>has sixty seconds:
>>twenty-one
>>twenty-two,
>>twenty-three,
>>twenty-four,
>>and so on.

Every hour has sixty minutes,
every day twenty-four hours,
and every week seven days.
It is the time
that is projected in space.
My past is very far away
behind me;
my future is very far away too
in front of me.
It is the time in which every hour
has the same length;
it is the time in which we can
indicate
dates and years.
But then there is another time,
our own psychological time,
the time in which we live,
in which a minute can last a century,
and five hours hardly a second.
Take your own experience
as an example.
You have to leave on a Kenya bus;
the bus is ready,
the motor is turning,
you need a ticket from the counter
at the office.
The man behind the counter tells you:
"I have to drink this coffee
first;
wait a second."
And outside the bus threatens
to leave,
the driver is hooting,
the passengers are waving
at you.
You have to wait,
half a minute,
one minute,
two minutes,

and it all seems to last
a hundred years,
eternity.
And then you go to a party,
a real swinging beautiful party
in lively company,
full of joy and swing.
You arrive,
you enjoy it,
you dance,
you drink,
you eat,
you chat,
and then your boy friend
or your girl friend comes to you
and whispers in your ear:
"Shouldn't we go home?
It is already two in the morning."
And you say:
"Two in the morning?
We came in only a minute ago."
You forgot the time.
It is in this psychological time
that Christians
can be so shocked
by the situations
in which they have to live
that they feel
that Jesus has to come back
very soon
to rule the nations
with fairness.

     Don't you think
     that Christians who are persecuted
     might expect him very soon
     because of that?
That soonness
is not so much connected
with a date:

December,
January,
1980,
or 2000,
but with their hope
and their belief.
And we too
should have something of that hope
and that belief;
the end is near;
he is coming soon.
We should not
sit down,
fold our hands,
and wait.
Paul did not do that;
Jesus did not do that either.
We should go on,
working
and building,
doing the things
that really matter,
because
the end
is near,
very near.

54.

A KINGDOM AS SECURITY

(Luke 23:35–43)

Not so very long ago,
some four hundred miles from here,
a truckload of men were unloaded
in front of a row of oildrums
filled with sand.
They were blindfolded,
they were bound to the drums,
and after that they were
shot,
one by one.
There are reports on how
those men died
in Uganda.
They were singing,
they were singing:
    "Do what you will,
      you have the power to kill,
      we did not do what you said
      we did.
      God is seeing us,
      God is seeing you,

God is knowing us,
God is knowing you.
God will judge us both:
we are his men."
And the last voice fell dead
only when the last man was shot.
Today is the last Sunday
of the year,
the Sunday of the last things,
the Sunday of death and resurrection,
the Sunday of the feast
of Jesus Christ,
universal king.
I think that in very many churches
today
preachers do not know
what to preach about.
They will ask each other,
what shall we say?
The time of kings is past;
the queens that last
are getting too expensive
to be maintained.
The time of the bosses is past,
we live in democratic days,
there are free elections,
we share our responsibilities,
there is team spirit,
nobody should be called superior
anymore.
Long live women's liberation,
let us hope for the men's one too;
we are republicans,
or we are democrats,
what is the difference?
We are free;
who are you
to tell us what to do?

Away with paternalism,
away with colonialism,
away with imperialism,
away with the administration,
away with examinations,
away with power,
it corrupts,
la luta continua
and so on.
And all that is beautiful,
but it is also a kind of daydream,
because there is still colonialism,
because there is still imperialism,
because there is still oppression,
because there are still people
standing in front of judges,
because there are still the oppressed,
because there are still the poor
and the landless
and the vagrants
and the unemployed
and us, ourselves.
It is all there in a big way;
it is all there in a small way:
the pushing and the pulling,
the stealing and the bribing,
the buying of a body
for the price of a bottle of beer,
the stealing of telephone time,
the backbiting and the gossip.
If we human beings
were delivered
unconditionally
into the hands of each other
without any further ado,
there would be not too much hope,
I am afraid.

And that is why
all those people led
to their execution
in the beginning of this sermon
were proudly shouting,
according to a very old African custom:
"I am his,
I am God's,
I am his woman,
I am his man,
he made me,
he will judge,
and he will watch!"
They were invoking God's supreme kingship,
his overall might.
From of old that kingship of God,
has been our
      guarantee,
      hope,
      and security.
We celebrate his kingship today
with a report of how he hung on the cross.
Where is his power,
where is his might,
where is our security,
where is our guarantee?
      The high priests came to him,
      and they had
      that very same question:
         "Hey, you, up there,
         what power do you have?
         If you are the son of God,
         save yourself."
      And he did not answer.
And then the soldiers came,
and they shouted
the very same question:

"Hey, you up there,
if you are a king,
save yourself."
And he did not answer.
       And then the murderer
       next to him
       turned to him
       and shouted,
       overbridging the distance
       between their crosses,
       the very same question:
       "Hey, you, over there,
       if you are the Christ,
       save yourself."
       And he did not answer.
And then the other murderer spoke up.
He did not shout;
he simply said:
"Please, Sir,
think of me.
I am hanging here for a good reason;
I deserve it.
You,
you know
how this happened to me.
Please, Sir,
think of me,
when you are in your kingdom."
And Jesus turned to him,
he answered him,
and he said:
       "I promise you,
       today you will be with me
       in paradise."
That is what his kingdom is about,
thinking about others,
thinking about us.

If God were not thinking of us,
where would we be?
> Love is our substance,
> his love is our substance,
> it should be our substance
> in all and everything.
> His love is our security
> and guarantee.
> Alleluia
> AMEN.

INDEX OF SCRIPTURAL TEXTS